ANTON CHEKHOV

Born in provincial Russia in 1860, Chekhov first turned to writing as a medical student in Moscow University, from which he graduated in 1884. His early plays were mostly short monologues and one-act farces such as *The Bear*, *The Proposal* and *The Wedding*. These achieved considerable popularity, but his first three full-length plays to be staged, *Ivanov* (1887), *The Wood Demon* (1889) and *The Seagull* (1896) were initially failures. Success came only when the Moscow Art Theatre under Stanislavsky revived *The Seagull* two years later and followed it with Chekhov's masterpieces, *Uncle Vanya* (1899), *Three Sisters* (1901) and *The Cherry Orchard* in 1904, which was the year of his death from consumption.

CORDELIA LYNN

Cordelia Lynn is a playwright and librettist. Plays include *Three Sisters* (Almeida Theatre); *One For Sorrow*, *Lela & Co.* (Royal Court Theatre); *Best Served Cold* (VAULT Festival). Opera includes *Miranda* (Opéra Comique). Other vocal work includes *Heave* (Festival Royaumont); *The White Princess* (Festival d'Aix-en-Provence); *you'll drown, dear* (Festival Manifest). Daramaturgy includes *Lucia di Lammermoor* (Royal Opera House). Cordelia was awarded the Harold Pinter Commission in 2017. Her play *Hedda Tesman*, after Henrik Ibsen's *Hedda Gabler*, will premiere in summer 2019 (Headlong, Chichester Festival and UK tour).

Anton Chekhov

THREE
SISTERS

A Drama in Four Acts

in a new version by
Cordelia Lynn

NICK HERN BOOKS
London
www.nickhernbooks.co.uk

A Nick Hern Book

This version of *Three Sisters* first published as a paperback original in Great Britain in 2019 by Nick Hern Books Limited, The Glasshouse, 49a Goldhawk Road, London W12 8QP

This version of *Three Sisters* copyright © 2019 Cordelia Lynn

Cordelia Lynn has asserted her right to be identified as the author of this version

Cover photograph: Patsy Ferran, Pearl Chanda and Ria Zmitrowicz, photographed by Nadav Kander

Designed and typeset by Nick Hern Books, London
Printed in Great Britain by Mimeo Ltd, Huntingdon, Cambridgeshire PE29 6XX

A CIP catalogue record for this book is available from the British Library

ISBN   978 1 84842 860 7

Woodland
CARBON
www.woodlandcarbon.co.uk
NICK HERN BOOKS
Printed on Carbon Captured paper

This version of *Three Sisters* was first performed at the Almeida Theatre, London, on 16 April 2019 (previews from 6 April), with the following cast:

MASHA SERGEYEVNA	Pearl Chanda
NATASHA IVANOVNA	Lois Chimimba
VASILY VASILEVICH SOLYONY	Alexander Eliot
OLGA SERGEYEVNA	Patsy Ferran
ANFISA	Annie Firbank
FYODOR ILYICH KULYGIN	Elliot Levey
FERAPONT	Eric MacLennan
ALEXANDER IGNATEVICH VERSHININ	Peter McDonald
ANDREY SERGEYEVICH	Freddie Meredith
VLADIMIR	Sonny Poon Tip
NIKOLAY LVOVICH TUZENBACH	Shubham Saraf
ALEXEY (LITTLE ALEX)	Akshay Sharan
IVAN ROMANOVICH CHEBUTYKIN	Alan Williams
IRINA SERGEYEVNA	Ria Zmitrowicz

Direction	Rebecca Frecknall
Design	Hildegard Bechtler
Lighting	Jack Knowles
Sound	George Dennis
Composition	Angus MacRae
Casting	Julia Horan CDG
Costume Supervision	Laura Hunt
Prop Supervision	Lizzie Frankl
Resident Director	Ebenezer Bamgboye
Associate Lighting Designer	Jamie Platt

ALMEIDA
THEATRE

The Almeida Theatre makes brave new work that asks big questions: of plays, of theatre and of the world around us.

Whether new work or reinvigorated classics, the Almeida brings together the most exciting artists to take risks; to provoke, inspire and surprise our audiences.

Recent highlights include Rupert Goold's Olivier Award-winning production of *Ink* (transferred to the West End and transfers to Broadway in 2019), Robert Icke's productions of *Hamlet* (transferred to the West End and was broadcast on BBC TWO), *Mary Stuart* (transferred to the West End and toured the UK) and Rebecca Frecknall's production of *Summer and Smoke* (transferred to the West End).

Other notable productions have included *American Psycho: a new musical thriller* (transferred to Broadway); *Chimerica* (won three Olivier Awards and transferred to the West End); *King Charles III* (won the Olivier Award for Best New Play and transferred to the West End and Broadway, toured the UK and Sydney, and was adapted into a BAFTA nominated TV drama); and *Oresteia* (transferred to the West End and won the Olivier Award for Best Director).

Patsy Ferran in *Summer and Smoke* by Tennessee Williams, directed by Rebecca Frecknall at the Almeida Theatre (2018). Photo by Marc Brenner.

almeida.co.uk

Artistic Director **Rupert Goold**

Executive Director **Denise Wood**

Associate Directors **Robert Icke, Rebecca Frecknall**

🐦 @AlmeidaTheatre

📘 /almeidatheatre

📷 @almeida_theatre

Registered Charity no. 282167

Supported using public funding by
**ARTS COUNCIL
ENGLAND**

Principal Partner

ASPEN

Play In Between: An Author's Note

I worked from Helen Rappaport's literal translation to create this
script, which sits somewhere strange between a translation and an
adaptation. The idea is to offer Anton Chekhov's *Three Sisters* to
a modern, English-speaking audience while remaining as faithful
as possible to his substance and style. Consequently, I haven't
modernised or relocated it but have mostly played with language
and rhythm.

The main exception to this is in the quotations which occur
throughout the play. I felt that a writer's use of quotation to
indicate meaning to their local audience demanded a culturally
relatable alternative for my own audience. The hope is to
translate the moment of recognition and subsequent feeling, an
idea which sits somewhere strange between being truthful and
being faithful. The quotations are marked in the text, with the
originals given in an appendix.

This *Three Sisters* exists in a liminal space between past and
present, Russian and Western, foreignising and domesticating,
and my choices regarding names reflect that. I didn't want to
rename the characters or cut the patronymics and nicknames
altogether, as I believe they are profoundly embedded in the
texture of the play. Adaptations I made for ease of Western eyes
and ears are as follows: The male characters are called by their
given rather than their family names, and Mariya Sergeyevna
and Natalya Ivanovna are Masha and Natasha throughout. Some
patronymics have been cut to facilitate English speech patterns,
and indicate relationships developing from formal to informal.
Alexey has been given the nickname 'Little Alex' to avoid
confusion with Alexander Ignatevich, a choice inspired by his
family name in the original, Fedotik, a diminutive meaning
'Little Fedo'.

C.L.

Characters

PROZOROV FAMILY
ANDREY SERGEYEVICH (Andryusha, Andryushka)
OLGA SERGEYEVNA (Olya, Olechka, Olyushka) ⎫
MASHA SERGEYEVNA (Mashenka) ⎬ *his sisters*
IRINA SERGEYEVNA (Irinka) ⎭
ANFISA, *an old nanny*

LOCALS
NATASHA IVANOVNA, *Andrey's lover, later his wife*
FYODOR ILYICH KULYGIN (Fedya), *Masha's husband,*
a teacher
FERAPONT, *employee of the local council*

THE SOLDIERS
ALEXANDER IGNATEVICH VERSHININ,
Lieutenant-Colonel
NIKOLAY LVOVICH TUZENBACH, *Lieutenant, a baron*
VASILY VASILEVICH SOLYONY, *Junior Captain*
IVAN ROMANOVICH CHEBUTYKIN, *Army Doctor,*
Prozorov tenant
ALEXEY (Little Alex), *Second Lieutenant*
VLADIMIR, *Second Lieutenant*

And a MAID, SOLDIERS, BUSKERS

The action takes place in a provincial town, over a period of roughly three years.

Note on Text

A forward slash (/) indicates an interruption.

This text went to press before the end of rehearsals and so may differ slightly from the play as performed.

ACT ONE

Midday. Spring. Sun. Light.

The Prozorovs' house. A living room with a large hall beyond. The table in the hall is being laid for lunch.

In the living room, OLGA *in navy,* MASHA *in black,* IRINA *in white.*

OLGA. Daddy died a year ago today. Exactly a year ago, the fifth of May, on your birthday. Irina. It was cold. It was snowing. You fainted – do you remember? – and I thought I wasn't going to survive but here we are a whole year later and we can talk about it like it was –

Look at you now. You're wearing white again. You're radiant.

The clock strikes twelve.

The clock struck twelve just like that.

Pause.

I remember when they carried him out of the church the military band was playing, and the soldiers fired a salute at the graveside. But even though he was a general there weren't many people, at the funeral I mean. Though it was raining. Heavy rain and snow /

IRINA. Why are you doing this?

NIKOLAY, IVAN *and* VASILY *come into the hall.*

OLGA. No leaves on the birch trees yet, but it's warm enough to keep the windows open… It was the beginning of May when we left Moscow too but everything was already in bloom. It was so hot, the city was rich in the sunshine. Then Daddy was given his brigade and we had to move here and although it was eleven years ago I remember it like it was yesterday…

God! I woke up this morning, I opened my eyes and my room was full of light, my room was full of the spring and I felt like I was filling up too and I longed, I longed to go home.

IVAN (*to* VASILY). Bollocks!

NIKOLAY (*to* VASILY). That doesn't make any sense.

MASHA (*whistles her song*).[1]

OLGA. Stop whistling Masha. It's annoying.

Pause.

It's just that I get these headaches. I go to school every morning and teach all day and my head aches and aches. My brain feels sort of crippled and my thoughts are sort of dead, like I'm old already... I've been working at that school for four years and for four years they've bled me dry, drop by drop, every day, but there's one thought left in me that gets clearer and clearer /

IRINA. Get out of here and go back to Moscow! Sell the house, settle up and go. To Moscow...

OLGA. Yes! Back to Moscow as soon as we can.

IVAN (*laughs*).   NIKOLAY (*laughs*).

IRINA. Andrey's going to be a professor anyway so he can't live here. The only thing stopping us is Masha...

OLGA. Masha will come and visit us every summer, for the whole summer.

MASHA (*softly whistles her song*).

IRINA. It'll all work out, you'll see. It's such a lovely day today! I feel like my lungs are expanding. When I woke up I remembered it was my birthday and I was so excited, like on my birthday when I was little and Mummy was still alive. I had such wonderful dreams...

OLGA. You're glowing today, you look beautiful. Masha is beautiful too. Andrey would be handsome but he's put on weight and it doesn't suit him. And I've got old and thin,

I suppose from being angry at the girls all day... But not today! Today I'm free, I'm at home, I don't have a headache, I actually feel my age again! I'm only twenty-eight after all... Everything happens for a reason, but sometimes I think I'd be happier if I got married and could stay at home all day.

Pause.

I would have loved my husband.

NIKOLAY (*to* VASILY). You're ridiculous, I'm sick of listening to you. (*Comes into the living room and sits at the piano.*) I've been meaning to tell you, our new battery commander is planning to visit today.

OLGA. Really?

IRINA. Is he old?

NIKOLAY. Not very. Mid-forties at most. (*Plays the piano as he speaks.*) He seems nice. Certainly not stupid, though he does talk a lot.

IRINA. Is he interesting?

NIKOLAY. Fairly. But he has a wife, a mother-in-law and two daughters, it's his second marriage too, and wherever he goes he says, 'I have a wife and two daughters.' He'll say it here, just you wait. Apparently she's sort of mad, the wife, does her hair in a long, thick plait like a little girl, talks politics and pseudo-intellectual stuff and every now and again tries to kill herself, apparently just to annoy her husband. I'd have done a runner long ago but he just complains about it to everyone.

VASILY *and* IVAN *come into the living room.* IVAN *is reading a magazine.*

VASILY (*at once*). With one arm I can lift sixteen kilos, / but with two arms I can lift fifty, even sixty kilos. Evidently two men are not twice as strong as one, but about three times, if not more...

IVAN (*at once*). For male pattern baldness... dissolve five grams of naphthalene in half a bottle of spirit... Use daily.

(*Writes in a little notebook*.) I'll make a note of that... So as I was saying, you just put a cork in a little bottle, run a glass tube through it, then you take the teeniest pinch of ordinary /

IRINA. Ivan Ivan Ivan!

IVAN. Yes, my love, light of my life?

IRINA. Why do I feel so happy today? Like I'm sailing in a great blue sky with great white birds all around me. Tell me why!

IVAN (*takes her hands and kisses them*). Little bird...

IRINA. I woke up this morning, I got out of bed, I got washed, and suddenly it was like I understood everything in the world and I knew how we're supposed to live. Trust me, I know *everything*. We have to work. Whoever we are we have to work and work hard otherwise we'll never be happy. If you don't work then you may as well not be alive, you may as well forget being a human being altogether! It's better to be an animal than a young woman who wakes up at twelve, has breakfast in bed then takes two hours to get ready. It's disgusting! You know how in hot weather you long for a glass of cold, clear water? That's how I long to work. And if I don't start getting up very early and working very hard then you have to promise never to speak to me ever again!

IVAN (*tender*). I promise, I promise...

OLGA. Daddy made us get up at seven every day. Now Irina still wakes at seven but she lies in bed for hours thinking and thinking. (*Laughs*.) And she has such a serious expression on her face!

IRINA. You still think I'm a little girl so you find it funny when I'm serious. But I'm twenty years old!

NIKOLAY. I understand you completely Irina. I come from a rich and privileged family that didn't have to work and never worried about anything. When I got home from cadet school an orderly used to take off my boots while I had some kind of a tantrum, but my mother spoilt me and was surprised if anyone thought I was anything less than miraculous. They tried to protect me from work, they hid me from it. But they didn't succeed, not quite! The world is changing, you can feel the weight of it building in the air. There's a great storm coming, coming closer and closer and it's going to break over all our laziness and indifference and apathy and cleanse the rotten heart right out of our society. I'm going to work, and in twenty-five or thirty years so will everyone else. Everyone!

IVAN. I won't.

NIKOLAY. You don't count.

VASILY. In twenty-five years you'll be dead. If you don't have a stroke first I'll crack and put a bullet in your brain. (*Takes out a bottle of perfume and perfumes his chest and his hands.*)

IVAN. But the truth is the moment I graduated I didn't do a thing. I even stopped reading, I haven't finished a book in years. All I read are these silly magazines. Look... (*A magazine.*) According to this magazine there was a critic called Dobrolyubov, but what he critiqued and why I haven't the foggiest...

Knocking from the floor below.

That's for me! It's for me. I'm expecting someone. I'll be back in a minute...

Exit IVAN.

IRINA. He's up to something...

NIKOLAY. He's obviously going to give you some kind of extravagant present.

IRINA. But I told him not to!

OLGA. Why is he always doing these embarrassing things /

MASHA (*standing, singing her song*). 'On a curved white shore grows a green oak tree, with a golden chain wound round and round... A golden chain wound round and round...'[2]

OLGA. You're in an odd mood today Masha.

MASHA, *humming, gets her hat.*

Where are you going?

MASHA. Home.

IRINA. Home!

NIKOLAY. But it's your sister's birthday!

MASHA. It doesn't matter, I'll be back this evening anyway.
(*Kisses* IRINA.) Bye for now darling, happy birthday…
When Daddy was still alive thirty or forty officers would
come and celebrate with us, it was so loud you couldn't hear
yourself think. Now there's about one and a half people and
it's silent as a desert… Okay I'm going. I'm feeling a little
down today, don't pay any attention to me. (*Laughs*.) We'll
catch up later, but I've got to get out /

IRINA. You're *so* /

OLGA (*upset*). It's okay Masha. I understand.

VASILY. If a man talks a lot then that's a lecture, or at least
a speech. But what do you call it when a woman talks a lot?

Beat.

MASHA. What do you *mean* you weird little man!

VASILY. Nothing. 'Little pig little pig, let me come in, No no
by the hair on my chinny chin chin!'[3]

Pause.

MASHA. Stop *crying* Olga!

ANFISA (*off*). This way old man. Come on in, your boots are
clean…

Enter ANFISA *and* FERAPONT *with a big pink cake on
a trolley.*

Look Irina, from the council, from Mikhail Ivanych
Protopopov… A cake!

IRINA. How nice. Will you thank him for me?

FERAPONT. What's that?

IRINA (*loud and clear*). I said please thank him for me!

OLGA. Nanny, give him a slice of cake. Go on Ferapont, they'll give you a slice of cake downstairs.

FERAPONT. You what?

ANFISA. Come along old man, let's go, cake time…

Exit ANFISA *and* FERAPONT *with the cake.*

MASHA. I don't like that Mikhail Ivanych Potty-popov or whatever he's called. You shouldn't have invited him.

IRINA. I didn't.

MASHA. Well that's alright then.

Enter IVAN *with a* SOLDIER *very much bearing aloft a silver samovar.*

IVAN. My dearest girls /

OLGA (*at once*). A samovar! A *silver* samovar! (*Escapes to the hall, upset.*) How much did that cost him?

IRINA (*at once*). Oh my god…

NIKOLAY (*at once, laughing*). Told you!

MASHA. Ivan Romanych are you insane?

Beat.

IVAN. My dearest, sweetest girls. You're all I have in the world. To me you're the most precious… I'm going to be sixty soon and soon I'm going to be an old man, a lonely insignificant old –

What I'm trying to say is there's nothing good left in me except for my love for you, and if it weren't for you I'd have given up long ago… (*To* IRINA.) My little bird, I've known you since the day you were born, I carried you in my arms the day you were born… I loved your late mother /

IRINA. But you can't give me such expensive presents!

IVAN. Expensive presents? Get out! (*To the* SOLDIER.) Get it out of here!

The SOLDIER *takes the samovar into the hall and leaves.*

'Expensive presents!'

Enter ANFISA, *talking as she crosses the room.*

ANFISA. Girls, a colonel we don't know has just arrived downstairs. He's already taken his coat off and he's coming up here to meet you. Irinka, you be on your best behaviour won't you... And it's well past lunchtime and nobody's even sat down to eat, oh dear oh dear...

Exit ANFISA *on the other side, still talking.*

NIKOLAY. That'll be Vershinin.

Enter ALEXANDER.

(*Stands.*) Lieutenant-Colonel.

ALEXANDER. Afternoon. (*To* IRINA *and* MASHA.) Alexander Ignatevich Vershinin. I'm delighted to see you again... But you're all grown up!

IRINA. Thank you for coming, please sit down.

ALEXANDER. I'm delighted, really delighted... But. Weren't there three of you? I remember three little girls. I don't remember your faces exactly, but I'm sure Colonel Prozorov had three little girls, I distinctly remember seeing you there, sitting in a row... How time flies!

NIKOLAY. Alexander Ignatevich is from Moscow.

IRINA. Moscow? You're from Moscow?

ALEXANDER. That's right, I was an officer in the same brigade as your father. (*To* MASHA.) Now your face I think do remember...

MASHA. Well I don't remember yours.

IRINA. Olya! Olya come back! The new colonel is from Moscow!

OLGA *comes into the living room.*

ALEXANDER. So you're Olga Sergeyevna, the eldest...
You're Masha... And you must be the youngest, Irina...

OLGA. You're really from Moscow?

ALEXANDER. Yes. I trained and served there for a long time
but now I've been given my own battery here – so here I am.
I don't remember you individually, I just remember there were
three of you. Three sisters. Your father, on the other hand,
I just have to close my eyes and I can see him, like he's
standing alive in front of me. I used to visit you in Moscow...

OLGA. And I thought I remembered everyone...

ALEXANDER. My full name is Alexander / Ignatevich

IRINA. Alexander Ignatevich from Moscow!

OLGA. We're moving there you know /

IRINA. We'll be there by the autumn. It's our home town, we
were born there.

They laugh, happy.

MASHA. It's so unexpected, someone from home... Wait!
Wait! Now I remember! Don't you remember Olya,
everyone used to joke about the Lovesick Major? You were
still a lieutenant then and you were in love with someone,
and everyone used to tease you by calling you Major...

ALEXANDER (*laughs*). That's right. That's me... the Lovesick
Major...

MASHA. You didn't have a beard then... You've really aged!

ALEXANDER. Well, when I was the Lovesick Major I was
young and in love. Not any more.

OLGA. But you don't have a single grey hair. He's aged but
he's not old.

ALEXANDER. All the same, I'm turning forty-three this year.
Have you been away from Moscow long?

IRINA. Eleven years... Masha why are you crying! Oh no, now
I'm going to cry too...

MASHA. Just ignore me. And where did you live?

ALEXANDER. Old Basmannaya Street.

OLGA. So did we! We were born there…

ALEXANDER. Later I moved to Nemetskaya Street. From there when you walk to the Red Barracks you have to cross a dark little bridge. If you stop and stand still you can hear the water rushing away beneath you. It's a sad place for a man to be alone.

Pause.

But here! Here you have a wonderful wide river, a real river!

OLGA. Yes but it's always cold. It's cold and there are millions of mosquitoes.

ALEXANDER. No! It's a good, healthy climate here. The forest, the river… And so many birch trees. Lovely humble birches, my favourite trees. It's a nice place to live. The only strange thing is that the station is twenty kilometres out of town… And no one seems to know why.

VASILY. I do.

Everyone looks at him.

Because if the station were near then it wouldn't be far, and if it's far then it can't be near.

Awkward silence.

NIKOLAY. Our resident joker, Vasily Vasilich…

OLGA. I've remembered you now. I remember…

ALEXANDER. I knew your mother.

IVAN. A wonderful woman.

IRINA. Mummy is buried in Moscow.

OLGA. When we move back we're going to put flowers on her grave.

MASHA. But I'm already beginning to forget her face, it's terrible... I suppose people won't remember us either. They'll forget us.

ALEXANDER. Yes. They'll forget. But that's life, there's nothing to be done about it. Everything we think is serious, meaningful and important will be forgotten, or eventually won't seem important at all.

Pause.

The strange thing is we can't know what will or won't be considered meaningful and important in the future. In Copernicus's or Columbus's own time everyone thought their discoveries were useless, absurd, heretical even, and that some empty rubbish written by some empty nutter was the truth. Maybe one day our own lives too will be looked back on as strange, uncomfortable, stupid, unhygienic, *wrong* even...

NIKOLAY. Who knows? Maybe they'll say we lived elevated lives and remember us with respect. Torture and capital punishment are illegal now, we're not fighting any wars... But there's still so much suffering!

VASILY. Blah blah blah... Don't give the Baron any lunch, he lives off hot air.

NIKOLAY. Leave me alone Vasily Vasilich... It's getting boring.

VASILY. Blah blah blah...

NIKOLAY. But doesn't the fact that we acknowledge this suffering demonstrate social progress, when poverty and sickness used to be considered normal, even acceptable?

ALEXANDER. Yes. Yes of course.

IVAN. You just said they'll think our lives were elevated, but human beings themselves are so small. (*Stands.*) Look how small I am. You have to say my life is elevated to make me feel better.

ANDREY *plays the violin.*

MASHA. That's our brother Andrey playing!

IRINA. He's the clever one! He's going to be a professor. Daddy was a military man but his son wanted to be an academic /

MASHA. It was Daddy's idea /

OLGA. He's sulking because we've been teasing him today. It seems he's a little in love...

IRINA. With a local girl. She'll be here for lunch, probably /

MASHA. Urgh but just wait till you see her clothes! It's not that they're ugly or unfashionable, they're just *weird*. All these bright, clashing colours, and so much make-up! Andrey isn't in love, he does have some taste after all. He's just trying to annoy us. Besides, I hear she's going to marry Protopopov, he's the Chairman of the Local Council. Well good luck to them, they're perfectly matched... (*Calls*.) Andrey!

ANDREY *stops playing the violin.*

Andrey come here a minute! Just for a minute!

Enter ANDREY. *He is sweating. He has a handkerchief with which he wipes his face and hands.*

OLGA. This is our brother, Andrey Sergeich.

ALEXANDER. Vershinin.

ANDREY. Prozorov. So you're the new battery / commander?

OLGA. Alexander Ignatich is from Moscow!

ANDREY. Really? Congratulations. Now my sisters will never leave you alone.

ALEXANDER. I'm sure they're bored of me already /

IRINA. Look at this little picture frame Andrey gave me for my birthday! (*A frame*.) He made it himself!

ALEXANDER. That's... A very nice frame.

IRINA. And that big one there, on the piano, he made that one too /

OLGA. He's not just the clever one, he's the talented one.

ANDREY *tries to slip out.*

He plays the violin, and he makes all sorts of things, he can really do anything he sets his mind to... Andrey come back! He's always sneaking off...

MASHA *and* IRINA *bring* ANDREY *back.*

MASHA. Back you come!

ANDREY. Please let me go...

MASHA. You're so sensitive! Everyone used to call Alexander Ignatevich the Lovesick Major and he didn't mind.

ALEXANDER. Not at all!

MASHA. And now I'm going to call you the Lovesick Violinist!

IRINA. Or the Lovesick Professor!

OLGA. He's in love! Andryusha's in love!

IRINA. Andryushka's in love he's in love he's in love!

IVAN (*sneaks up behind* ANDREY *and grabs him*). 'Andrey and Natasha sitting in a tree...'[4]

ANDREY. Okay stop now stop... I said stop!

Beat.

(*Wipes his face.*) I didn't sleep last night and I'm feeling a little... I was reading till four in the morning and when I went to bed these thoughts were just going round and round in my head... And the sun comes up so early here it just creeps into the bedroom... I'm planning to translate a book from the English this summer but /

ALEXANDER. You read English?

ANDREY. Oh yes. Our father, bless him, piled what he called 'a proper education' on us. I know it sounds silly but after he died I began to put on weight, like my body had been liberated... Thanks to him we know French, German and English, and Irina knows Italian too. But it cost so much...

MASHA. Knowing three languages in this place is an
unnecessary luxury. No, worse, it's like some superfluous...
I don't know, like a sixth finger or something. We know a lot
of useless things.

ALEXANDER. Useless things? (*Laughs.*) You know a lot of
useless things? But I don't think there's anywhere in the
world, or ever could be anywhere in the world, that doesn't
need intelligent and educated people. Let's say that in a
population of one hundred thousand in this backward and
uncultured town there are only three people lucky enough to
be educated like you. Well of course you can't compete with
all the ignorance that surrounds you. Day by day, little by
little, you'll give way, you'll diminish, until one day you'll
vanish in the dark mass of the crowd. Yes, life is going to
swallow you whole, but you won't disappear altogether
because of the influence you'll have had. After you're gone
maybe another six people like you will appear, then twelve
and so on and so on until one fine day thoughtful, educated
people are the majority and life will be unimaginably
beautiful. This beautiful future isn't going to be today, but we
need to sense that it's coming, we have to wait for it, dream of
it, believe in it. That's why it's our duty to see more and know
more than our parents and grandparents saw and knew.
(*Laughs.*) And you're complaining about your education!

MASHA (*takes off her hat*). I'm staying for lunch.

IRINA. Wow... Someone should have written all that down...

ANDREY *has vanished*.

NIKOLAY. I agree that in the future life will be beautiful. But
you *can* take part in it now, even from this distance you can
prepare for it, you have to work /

ALEXANDER. Yes. But look at all these flowers! And what
a lovely house. Your father's old quarters? I'm jealous. I've
spent my whole life creeping about in poky little quarters
with a few chairs and one sofa, and the stoves always smoke.
I've never had flowers like these in my home... Ah well...

NIKOLAY. I'm telling you, you have to work. You're probably
thinking that the German has got all emotional, but actually
I'm as Russian as you are and I don't even speak German.
So...

Pause.

ALEXANDER. Do you ever wonder what would happen if we
could live our lives all over again but be fully conscious of it
the second time? I bet we'd try to do everything differently, or
at least would know to create a different world for ourselves,
somewhere like this surrounded by flowers and light... I have
a wife and two little girls, and on top of that my wife is.
Unwell... But if I could live my life again I definitely
wouldn't get married! Oh no!

Enter FYODOR.

FYODOR. Dearest little sister! Many congratulations to you on
your birthday! I wish you sincerely, from the bottom of my
heart, health and happiness and everything a young lady of
your age could desire. Allow me to present, by way of a
humble gift, this little book. (*A book.*) The history of our
very own secondary school, written by: me. It's just a small
thing, practically inconsequential, scribbled in my idle
hours... But read it anyway. (*To the room.*) Afternoon
everyone! (*To* ALEXANDER.) Fyodor Ilyich Kulygin,
classics teacher at our secondary school. (*Back to* IRINA.)
In this insignificant chronicle you'll find a list of all our
graduates from the past fifty years. Isn't that interesting?
Feci quod potui, faciant meliora potentes. (*Kisses* MASHA.)
I have done what I could, let those who can do more.[5]

IRINA. But you gave me this for Easter.

FYODOR. No! Did I? (*Laughs.*) Well give it back then, or, yes,
give it to the Colonel. Take it, Colonel. Read it some time
when you've got nothing better to do.

ALEXANDER. Thank you. (*Stands.*) Well I'm so pleased
to have /

OLGA. You're leaving? No don't go!

IRINA. You have to stay and have lunch with us!

OLGA. Yes please stay!

ALEXANDER (*laughs*). Well if you insist... I seem to have interrupted your birthday party. I'm sorry, I didn't know and didn't congratulate you.

Goes into the hall with OLGA.

FYODOR. Sunday at last, the day of rest! And so we shall rest, and we shall make merry, each according to their age, circumstances, inclinations... It's finally spring, the carpets will be taken up for the summer and put away till the winter... With mothballs and insect powder... The Romans were healthy because they knew how to work but they also knew how to relax, they had *mens sana in corpore sano*, healthy minds in healthy bodies, and their lives flowed within defined forms. Our headmaster says that the most important thing in life is *form*. A thing which loses its form comes to its end, even in our everyday lives. (*Puts his arm around* MASHA, *laughing*.) Masha loves me, my wife loves me. The curtains, also, should be put away with the carpets... I'm happy today, I'm in an excellent mood. Masha, we need to be at the headmaster's by four, he's arranged a little outing for the teachers and their /

MASHA. I'm not going.

FYODOR. You're not going? Why?

MASHA. I'll tell you later /

FYODOR. But Masha /

MASHA. Okay okay, I'll go! (*Moves away*.) But please just leave me alone...

FYODOR. Excellent. After which we'll go back to the headmaster's for dinner. Despite his old age that man is above all things a sociable man, an inspiration. Yesterday after the meeting, he said to me: 'I'm tired, Fyodor Ilyich! Tired!'

Beat.

That clock is seven minutes fast. Yes, he said, 'I'm tired.' Extraordinary.

ANDREY *plays the violin.*

Enter OLGA.

OLGA. Lunch is ready! We're having pie.

FYODOR. Here you are, dear Olga! You know, yesterday I worked from first thing in the morning till eleven at night, I'm completely exhausted and I'm still so happy! (*They go into the hall together.*) Dearest Olga...

IVAN. Pie? Excellent!

MASHA. Just make sure you don't drink anything. Do you hear me? It's bad for you to drink /

IVAN. Bollocks to that, it's two years since I had any trouble with drinking. Anyway, who do you think you are? My mother?

MASHA. All the same, don't you dare drink!

IVAN. It really doesn't matter /

MASHA. I said don't you dare! (*Soft.*) Fuck it. Another evening being bored to death at the headmaster's.

NIKOLAY. Don't go. Simple.

IVAN. Yes, don't go darling.

NIKOLAY. I wouldn't if I were you /

MASHA. Oh 'Don't go don't go!' I hate my life.

Goes into the hall with IVAN.

IVAN. Come on now!

VASILY (*on his way to the hall*). Blah blah blah...

NIKOLAY. Stop it Vasily!

VASILY. Blah blah blah...

FYODOR (*a toast*). Welcome, Colonel! I'm a teacher by profession but in this house I can be myself, Masha's husband... She's a really good person, a really really good person...

ALEXANDER (*a toast*). Good health! (*To* OLGA.) It's so nice to be here with you!

IRINA *and* NIKOLAY *alone in the living room.*

IRINA. Masha's depressed again... She got married at eighteen when she thought Fyodor was the most intelligent man in the world. She doesn't think that any more. He is the kindest, but not the most intelligent...

OLGA. Andrey! Lunch!

ANDREY *stops playing the violin.*

ANDREY (*off*). Coming!

Enter ANDREY. *He goes to the hall.*

NIKOLAY. What are you thinking about?

IRINA. Nothing. I don't like that friend of yours, Vasily. I'm sort of afraid of him to be honest. When he talks he doesn't make any sense.

NIKOLAY. He can be a bit weird. I find him annoying but feel sorry for him at the same time... Mostly I feel sorry for him. I think he's shy... When we're alone together he can be really funny and nice, but when other people are around he goes strange, gets argumentative... Don't go! Wait until they've all sat down at least. Let me be with you for a moment... What are you thinking about?

Pause.

You're twenty, I'm not quite thirty. It's amazing to think how much life we have left to live, so many days, day after day, full of my love for /

IRINA. Nikolay. Don't.

NIKOLAY. Sometimes I'm overwhelmed by this feeling, a thirst, a yearning, to live, to struggle, to work, and this feeling has folded somehow with my feelings for you. Irina. Because you're beautiful, life is beautiful too... What are you thinking about?

IRINA. Maybe life seems beautiful to you, but for me and my sisters it hasn't been very beautiful. It's choked us, like weeds... I'm going to cry. Stop it. (*Stops. Smiles.*) We need to do something, really do something that makes a difference. That's why we're unhappy, because we don't have work that we care about. We were born into a world that hates work and doesn't care about anything...

Enter NATASHA. *A pink dress and a green belt.*

NATASHA. They've sat down already... I'm late... (*A mirror.*) Hair alright at the back... Irina! Happy birthday! (*Kisses her emphatically.*) You have so many guests! I feel all self-conscious... Hello Baron.

OLGA (*coming in*). Here you are Natasha! How are you?

They kiss. NIKOLAY *and* IRINA *to the hall.*

NATASHA. I didn't know it was a big party, I'm sort of embarrassed /

OLGA. Don't say that, we're all family and friends. (*Soft.*) But Natasha, you're wearing a green belt!

NATASHA. So? Is it bad luck?

OLGA. No, it just looks a bit weird, with the dress I mean...

They go into the hall.

NATASHA (*upset*). It does? But it isn't really green is it? More of a metallic neutral dull colour, don't you think?

Everyone at the table in the hall. The living room is empty.

FYODOR (*a toast*). Happy birthday Irina! Here's to finding a nice young man!

IVAN. Don't forget Natasha Ivanovna, she needs a nice young man too.

FYODOR. I thought Natasha Ivanovna already had a nice young man.

Laughter.

MASHA (*taps her glass with her knife*). More wine please! Live fast, die young, that's what I say.

FYODOR. C-minus for behaviour Masha…

ALEXANDER. This is delicious. What's it made of?

VASILY. Cockroaches.

IRINA. Eurgh-ugh… That's disgusting…

OLGA. It's so nice to be at home! We're having roast turkey and apple pie later, you should all stay for dinner.

ALEXANDER. Can I stay for dinner too?

IRINA. Yes please!

NATASHA. They're very informal here.

IVAN. 'Andrey and Natasha sitting in a / '

ANDREY. Stop it!

Laughter.

Enter ALEXEY *and* VLADIMIR *with a huge bouquet of flowers.* ALEXEY *has a camera.*

ALEXEY. Shit. They're already eating.

VLADIMIR. Are they? Shit. They are…

ALEXEY. Wait a second!

A photograph: the lunch party.

And just one more… Ha – that's excellent…

A photograph: VLADIMIR *posing with the flowers.*

Okay! Let's go.

They go into the hall with the flowers and are greeted noisily.

ALEXEY *and* VLADIMIR. 'Happy birthday to you! Happy birthday to you!'

ALL. 'Happy Birthday dear Irina, happy birthday to you-ou!'[6]

Applause.

VLADIMIR. Happy birthday darling! Isn't the weather glorious? Like a miracle. I was out walking all morning with the secondary-school boys. I've started teaching gymnastics there /

A photograph: the three sisters.

ALEXEY. You can move now Irina! (*Laughs.*) You look gorgeous by the way, really gorgeous...

A photograph: the soldiers.

And here, I've got a little present for you. It's a spinning top, it makes the most amazing sound. Listen...

The top sings through the house...

IRINA. Oh how beautiful...

... Softens...

... Settles...

MASHA (*sings soft*). 'On a curved white shore grows a green oak tree, with a golden chain wound round and round...

... Is silent.

'A golden chain wound round and...' Why am I singing that? I woke up singing and I can't get it out of my /

FYODOR. Thirteen! Thirteen people at the table!

VLADIMIR. I hope no one here is superstitious?

Laughter.

FYODOR. Thirteen at table means there are secret lovers... Not you I hope, doctor?

Laughter.

IVAN. The things I could tell you... But look! Natasha Ivanovna is blushing! I can't begin to imagine why...

Loud laughter.

NATASHA *runs into the living room,* ANDREY *after her.*

ANDREY. It's okay, just ignore them! Wait, please wait... Please /

NATASHA. I don't know what's wrong with me but they treat me like some kind of joke! I know it was rude to storm off I know it was but I couldn't take it I couldn't I – (*Cries.*)

ANDREY. Please don't cry, please don't. I promise they're just joking, they don't mean it. Really, they're all good kind people and they love me and they love you. Come over here, they can't see us over here…

NATASHA. All these posh people and these posh parties… Oh god I'm so ashamed…

ANDREY. You're so sweet. You're so young and so sweet and so beautiful. Please don't cry! Trust me, just trust me… It's like my heart is filling up and spilling over it's amazing… They can't see us! They can't, I promise. I don't know why I fell in love with you or when I fell in love with you, I don't know anything except that I want you to marry me. Please marry me! I love you I love you… Never was a girl so loved…

A photograph: ANDREY *and* NATASHA *kiss.*

ACT TWO

Evening. Dark. Cold. Winter.

Outside someone is playing an accordion. Festivities press in on the house. The living room and hall beyond. The wind roars in the stove.

Enter NATASHA *with a candle. She goes to* ANDREY*'s door and listens.*

NATASHA. Andryusha? What are you doing? Are you reading again? It's nothing, I just… (*Goes and opens another door, looks in, closes it.*) No candles in there at least…

Enter ANDREY, *with a book.*

ANDREY. What's wrong. Natasha?

NATASHA. I'm just checking if there are any candles burning. It's carnival so you have to keep an eye on the servants. Yesterday I came down in the middle of the night and there was a candle on the table. Right there. A *lit*. Candle. When I find out who left it… (*Puts her candle down on the table.*) What time is it?

ANDREY. Quarter past eight.

NATASHA. Olga and Irina still aren't back from work poor things. Olga said she had a meeting but Irina should be home from the telegraph office by now. I've told her to take better care of herself, 'Irina sweetie take better care of yourself!' that's exactly what I said to her. But does she listen? No. Quarter past eight? Andrey I think our little Bobik isn't well. He's all cold. Yesterday he had a temperature but today he's cold… I'm frightened!

ANDREY. I'm sure he's fine Natasha.

NATASHA. We should put him on a special diet just in case.
I'm really frightened… Is it true they've hired musicians for
the party tonight? Andryusha I don't think they should come.

ANDREY. I don't know… It's tradition at carnival time.

NATASHA. This morning our baby woke up and looked right at
me and he *smiled*. That means he recognised me. 'Hello
Bobik,' I said, 'Hello pumpkin!' and, you won't believe it, he
laughed. Actually laughed. Children understand us you
know, they understand everything perfectly. I'll tell them not
to let the musicians in.

ANDREY. Isn't that up to my sisters? It's their house after all.

NATASHA. You're right, it's their house too. I'll tell them
myself, they'll understand, they're so nice… (*Moves away.*)
You're having yogurt for supper, the doctor says you can
only eat yogurt if you're going to lose weight. (*Stops.*) Bobik
won't stop shivering. I'm worried it's the nursery. Maybe we
should put him in a different room until it gets warmer.
Irina's room is perfect for a baby, don't you think? It's nice
and dry and gets the sun all day. We should ask her and then
she can move in with Olga for the time being… It doesn't
matter to her anyway, she works all day, she only comes
home to sleep…

Pause. The wind roars in the stove.

Andrey sweetie… Say something.

ANDREY. I'm thinking… And. There's nothing to say.

Beat.

NATASHA. Yes I meant to tell you. Ferapont's come from the
council. He's been asking for you.

ANDREY (*yawns*). Tell him to come up.

*Exit NATASHA. ANDREY reads by the candle she's
forgotten.*

Enter FERAPONT, a winter coat.

Hello old man. What's wrong?

FERAPONT. Protopopov's sent a book for you and some papers to sign. Here...

A book and some papers.

ANDREY. Thanks. You should have come earlier, it's already dark.

FERAPONT. What's that?

ANDREY (*loud and clear*). I said it's dark!

FERAPONT. I know. It was light when I got here but they didn't let me in. 'Mr Prozorov's busy,' they said. Well if he's busy he's busy, I don't mind, I don't have anywhere else to go.

Pause.

What's that?

ANDREY. I didn't say anything. (*Flicks through the new book.*) Tomorrow's Saturday. No meetings on Saturday but I'll go in anyway... Find something to do. It's boring at home...

Pause.

Dear old Ferapont... Isn't it funny how life turns out? I was so bored today, and then I got out this book, notes from my old university lectures, and I couldn't stop laughing... I'm the Secretary of the Local Council and Protopopov is Chairman. I am the Secretary and Protopopov is Chairman and the most I can hope for is to one day be a member of that council! A member of the Local Council... And every night I dream I'm a professor at Moscow University, a world-famous scholar, the pride of all Russia.

FERAPONT. I don't know... I don't hear very well you know...

ANDREY. If you could then I don't think I'd be telling you this. I need to talk to someone but my wife doesn't understand and. I'm afraid of my sisters. That they'll laugh at me and I'll feel ashamed... I don't drink, I don't like bars or fancy restaurants, but I think if I could just sit for a while in Tyostov's or the Moscow Grand I'd be so happy.

FERAPONT. A contractor told me, in Moscow, some businessmen were eating pancakes. One of them ate forty pancakes and died. Just went and died. Forty or fifty, don't remember exactly.

ANDREY. You sit in one of the great Moscow restaurants, you don't know anyone, no one knows you. But you don't feel like a stranger. Here you know everyone and everyone knows you but you're a stranger... A stranger and you're all alone.

FERAPONT. You what?

Pause.

And the same contractor said, though he's probably taking the piss, he said that they're going to stretch a rope from one side of Moscow to the other.

Beat.

ANDREY. Why?

FERAPONT. I don't know. It's what he said.

ANDREY. He's lying. (*Reads his book.*) Have you ever been to Moscow?

FERAPONT (*after some thought*). No.

Pause.

Can I go now?

ANDREY. Yes. Thank you. Safe journey home.

Exit FERAPONT.

Safe journey home... (*Reads his book.*) Come back tomorrow and pick up the papers. Goodnight...

Pause.

He's gone.

The doorbell rings.

Yes. Things. Lots of things to do...

Stands, stretches, goes to his study and closes the door.

Empty stage. The candle burning. Somewhere in the house a woman is singing to the baby.

A MAID *comes in and lights the candles and lamps.*

MASHA (*off*). I don't know.

Enter MASHA *and* ALEXANDER.

Pause.

I don't know. I guess it's just what you're used to in the end. After Daddy died it took us a while to get used to not having orderlies around. But aside from habit I still think what I said is true. Maybe not in other places but in our town all the principled and honest people, the educated people, are the soldiers.

ALEXANDER. I want a cup of tea.

MASHA. They'll bring it soon. Daddy let me get married when I was just eighteen. I was sort of in awe of my husband because he was a teacher and I'd only just graduated. I thought he was so wise, so intelligent and important... That didn't last.

ALEXANDER. Yes... I can see that.

MASHA. But I'm not really talking about him, I've got used to him. I mean the people here generally. They're so intolerant and ignorant and rude. I hate it. It's offensive. When someone isn't compassionate, isn't thoughtful or polite I feel it physically, here. When I have to spend time with my husband's colleagues it actually hurts.

ALEXANDER. I see... But I think they're all the same, in this town anyway. All the same! Just listen to your local intellectual, civilian or military, he's sick of his wife, sick of his house, sick of his farm, sick of his horses... Humanity is distinguished from other animals by our ability to express our thoughts and feelings at a sublime level so, tell me, why do we aim so low in real life? Why?

MASHA. Why...

ALEXANDER. Why is he sick of his children, sick of his wife? And why are his children and wife sick of him?

MASHA. You're not in a very good mood today.

ALEXANDER. I'm sorry. I skipped lunch, haven't eaten a thing since breakfast… And one of my girls is ill and when my daughters are ill I get these waves of anxiety… I feel guilty that their mother is the way she is. God you should have seen her this morning. What a worthless human being. We started arguing the moment we woke up, by nine I couldn't take it any more, just walked out and slammed the door.

Pause.

I don't normally talk to people about this. But I can talk to you… Strange…

He touches her face. Then her lips. Then the inside of her lips.

Don't be angry with me. You're all I have…

Pause. The wind roars in the stove.

MASHA. Listen to the stove. The wind comes down the chimney and gets trapped there and roars. Before Daddy died it was just like that.

ALEXANDER. Are you superstitious?

MASHA. Yes.

ALEXANDER. Strange… (*Kisses her face.*) You are a miraculous, wonderful woman. I can see your eyes shining in the dark.

MASHA (*moves away*). There's a light over here /

ALEXANDER. I love. Love. Love… Your eyes. How you walk. I dream about your eyes, I dream about you walking and walking…

MASHA. I want to laugh but I'm frightened. Please stop talking, please… (*Soft.*) Or… Don't. Stop talking. Why does it matter? (*Covers her face.*) It doesn't matter to me… Someone's coming. Say something else…

NIKOLAY (*off*). I have a triple-barrelled surname, Baron Tuzenbach-Krone-Altschauer, but I'm Russian just like you.

Enter IRINA *and* NIKOLAY.

The only German left in me is my stubbornness. I walk you home every evening /

IRINA. I'm so tired!

NIKOLAY. And every evening, for ten years, twenty years, I'll walk you home until you ask me to stop. (*Sees* MASHA *and* ALEXANDER. *Happily:*) You're both here! Hello.

IRINA. Home. Finally... (*To* MASHA.) Just now before I finished work a woman came in. She wanted to send a telegram to her brother in Saratov to tell him that her son died today but she just couldn't remember the address. I had to send it without one, just to her brother in Saratov. She was crying. And I was cruel to her and I don't know why. 'I'm busy! I don't have time for this!' It was all so stupid... Are the musicians coming tonight?

MASHA. Yes.

IRINA. I need to sit down. I'm exhausted.

NIKOLAY (*smiling*). When you get home from work you look so small and sad...

Pause.

IRINA. I'm. So. Tired... No. I don't like working at the telegraph office. I don't like it at all...

MASHA. You've lost weight. (*Whistles.*) It makes you look younger, you look like a boy.

NIKOLAY. That's just her hairstyle.

IRINA. I need to find another job, this one isn't right. Everything I believed work could and should be is exactly what this job is not. Thoughtless, meaningless /

A knock on the floor below.

The doctor's knocking. (*To* NIKOLAY.) Please knock back darling I can't... I'm too tired to move...

NIKOLAY *knocks on the floor.*

He'll come up now... Masha. We need to stage an
intervention. Ivan and Andrey went to the club yesterday and
lost. Again. Andrey lost two hundred roubles.

MASHA. So what are we supposed to do about it?

IRINA. Two weeks ago: he lost. In December: he lost. Maybe
it's a good thing. The quicker he loses all our money then the
sooner we can pack up and get out of here *oh. My. God.*
I dream I'm in Moscow every night! I'm like a mad person.
(*Laughs*.) We're moving in June. That's still... February,
March, April, May... Almost half a year!

MASHA. Just don't let Natasha find out about the gambling.

IRINA. I don't think it matters to her.

> IVAN *comes into the hall. He has been sleeping. He combs his
> beard in front of a mirror, sits down and reads a magazine.*

MASHA. There he is... Has he paid his rent yet?

IRINA (*laughs*). Are you joking? Not for months. I think he's
forgotten.

MASHA (*laughs*). Look at him sitting there, like he owns the
place...

> *They all laugh.*

> *Pause.*

IRINA. You're unusually quiet today Alexander.

ALEXANDER. I'm hungry. And I'd like some tea. Some tea
some tea my kingdom for some tea! I haven't eaten since
breakfast...

IVAN. Irina Sergeyevna!

IRINA. Yes?

IVAN. Come here please. *Venez ici.*

> IRINA *goes to the hall and sits at the table with* IVAN.

I need to have you near me.

> IRINA *lays out a game of patience.*

ALEXANDER. Right. If we're going to be denied tea then we may as well have a conversation.

NIKOLAY. What about?

ALEXANDER. What about? Well… What about. The Future.

NIKOLAY. The Future? Alright. In the future people will fly around in the sky, women will wear trousers, maybe they'll discover and develop a new way of communicating, and after all that life will still be exactly the same. Difficult, incomprehensible, but happy. And even in a thousand years we'll still walk around saying, 'Oh, life is hard!' and we'll still be afraid of death and not want to die.

ALEXANDER. Hmm. How do I put this… The way I see it everything is changing all the time, little by little, is changing right now in front of our eyes and in a hundred years, or in a thousand, the exact length of time doesn't matter, life is going to be happy and beautiful. We're not going to live to see it of course, but we are living *for* it now. We work, we suffer, we are making it a reality. That is the whole purpose of our lives, and in that purpose lies our only chance at happiness.

MASHA (*laughs, soft*).

NIKOLAY. What's so funny?

MASHA. I don't know. I've been laughing all day. I woke up laughing.

ALEXANDER. We went to the same cadet school but I didn't go to the military academy. I do read a lot but I don't know how to choose the right books so I probably read all the wrong things. And the longer I live the more I want to know. My hair is going grey, I'll be an old man soon and I still know so little! So little… But the only important thing I do know I know with absolute certainty. There can be no happiness for our generation. There can't be, there won't be… We just have to work and work, happiness belongs to the future.

Pause.

If not me then my children, and my children's children.

ALEXEY and VLADIMIR *come into the hall with a guitar. They play and sing quietly.*

NIKOLAY. But what if I *am* happy?

ALEXANDER. You're not.

NIKOLAY (*laughs*). How can I convince you?

MASHA (*laughs, soft*).

NIKOLAY. Go on, you keep laughing! (*To* ALEXANDER.) Life doesn't change, not in one hundred or two hundred years, not in a million years. In its essentials it remains the same and the rest is just decoration. It follows its own mysterious laws which are nothing to do with you and which you could never understand anyway. Migrating birds, geese for example, fly and fly. Whatever profound or shallow thoughts they have going round and round in their heads, they keep on flying without knowing why or where. Let the thinkers think and the dreamers dream so long as they keep on flying...

MASHA. But there has to be some meaning to it all?

NIKOLAY. Meaning? Look, it's snowing. What's the meaning in that?

Pause.

MASHA. But I think we need meaning, or at least we need to search for it otherwise life is just. Empty. Never to know why geese fly, why children are born, why there are stars in the sky... You have to know why you're alive or everything is just nothing. Nothing blowing in the wind...

Pause.

ALEXANDER. Yes... The fact is, it's sad not to be young any more.

MASHA. Gogol said, 'It's a depressing world, my friends!'

NIKOLAY. And I say, 'It's impossible arguing with you, my friends.' I give up!

IVAN (*reading his magazine*). Balzac was married in Berdichev.

IRINA *sings softly with* ALEXEY *and* VLADIMIR.

That's interesting. I might write that down. (*Writes in his notebook.*) Baal-zak... wahz... mah-reed... ih-n... Ber-dee-che-vuh.

IRINA (*singing to* ALEXEY*'s melody*). 'Balzac was married in Berdichev...'

IVAN *reads his magazine.* IRINA *lays out another game. And the wind roars in the stove.*

NIKOLAY. Right. It's decided. Did you hear Masha, I've handed in my resignation.

MASHA. I heard. Pity. I don't like civilians.

NIKOLAY. It doesn't matter... (*Stands.*) Look, I'm not a handsome man, what kind of a soldier did I make? Anyway... It doesn't matter because I'm going to work. I'm going to work so hard I come home in the evening, collapse into bed from exhaustion and sleep the sleep of the just. (*Goes into the hall.*) At least people who work properly sleep properly!

ALEXEY (*to* IRINA). I went to that funny shop on Moscow Street and got you some colouring pencils and a little penknife.

IRINA. You've got used to treating me like a child but actually I'm an adult now and – Oh Little Alex! They're lovely!

ALEXEY. I got a penknife for myself too. Look, they're very clever... A big blade... a small blade... a third with a serrated edge... a tiny pair of tweezers, a tiny pair of scissors, and this little thing is for cleaning your nails...

VLADIMIR. Doctor, how old are you?

IVAN. Me? Thirty-two.

Laughter.

ALEXEY. Are you playing patience? I'll show you a different layout. (*Lays out the cards.*)

ANFISA *brings the samovar and chocolates into the hall and prepares the tea. Later,* NATASHA *comes in and fusses around the samovar, then* VASILY, *who sits at the table and eats all the chocolates. And the wind roars in the stove.*

ALEXANDER. That wind!

MASHA. I know! I'm sick of winter. I've forgotten what summer feels like.

IRINA. I'm going to win! That means we'll go to Moscow.

ALEXEY. No, you can't win. The eight's covering the two of spades, see? (*Laughs.*) That means you won't go to Moscow!

IVAN (*reading*). There's a smallpox epidemic in Northern China.

ANFISA. Masha dear, have some tea. (*To* ALEXANDER.) Please, have some tea Colonel, sir... I'm sorry, I forgot your name...

MASHA. Could you bring it to us Nanny? I don't want to go over there...

IRINA. Nanny!

ANFISA. Coming!

NATASHA (*to* VASILY). Babies understand everything perfectly you know. 'Heh-*loh* Bobik,' I said, 'Hello my little sweet!' And he *looked* at me. In a special way I mean. You think it's just the mother in me talking, but I promise you, he's an extraordinary child.

VASILY. If he were mine I'd fry him in a pan and eat him. (*Goes into the living room with a drink and sits alone in the corner.*)

NATASHA. Horrible man!

MASHA. I'll tell you what happiness is. It's not knowing if it's summer or winter. If I were in Moscow I bet I wouldn't notice the weather...

ALEXANDER. I've been reading the prison diaries of a French minister, convicted over the Panama affair. He writes about the birds he can see through his bars with such rapture and love, the same birds he never even noticed when he was a free man. Now he's been released of course he's forgotten them all over again. It'll be just like that when you're in Moscow, you won't even realise you're there. We're not meant to be happy and we never will be. We just have to long for it.

NIKOLAY. Where are the chocolates?

IRINA. Vasily ate them.

NIKOLAY. What, all of them?

ANFISA (*giving him tea*). There's a letter for you Colonel.

ALEXANDER. For me? (*Takes the letter.*) From my daughter… (*Reads the letter.*) Yes. Of course… I'm sorry Masha I have to go. I won't have any tea. (*Stands, upset.*) Always the same – !

MASHA. What's happened?

ALEXANDER (*soft*). My wife's tried to poison herself again. I have to go, I don't want anyone to – It's horrible, horrible… (*Kisses MASHA's hands.*) You're miraculous… I'll just slip out through there…

He's gone.

ANFISA (*giving MASHA tea*). Where's he going? I just brought his tea… Rude…

MASHA. Go away! You're always lurking about! (*Goes to the hall with her tea.*) I'm sick of you you… Old woman!

ANFISA. What's upset you little one?

ANDREY (*off*). Anfisa!

ANFISA. 'Anfisa!' He just sits in there all day…

Exit ANFISA.

MASHA. Let me sit down! (*Swipes at IRINA's cards.*) Covering the whole table with your stupid game. Just… drink your tea!

IRINA. Someone's in a bad mood…

MASHA. If I'm in a bad mood then don't talk to me... Don't touch me!

IVAN (*laughs*). Don't touch her she says, she says she doesn't want to be touched...

MASHA. And you're sixty years old but you just talk shit, you talk shit like a little boy!

NATASHA. Do you *have* to swear like that Masha? I'm telling you this for your own good, you're so pretty and you'd be even prettier if you didn't use such nasty language...

NIKOLAY (*starts giggling*).

NATASHA. *Je vous prie, pardonnez moi, Marie, mais vous avez des manières un peu grossières.*

Beat.

I'm learning French.

NIKOLAY (*dying*). Please... Please someone pass me... the brandy...

A baby cries somewhere in the house.

NATASHA. *Il parait que mon Bobik deja ne dort pas.* My baby's woken up, he's a little poorly today. Excuse me, I've got to go to him...

Exit NATASHA.

IRINA. Where's Alexander gone?

MASHA. Home. To his wife. She's not well.

NIKOLAY *goes to* VASILY.

NIKOLAY. You're always sitting on your own looking tormented. Come on, let's be friends. Have a brandy.

They drink.

I suppose I'll have to play the piano tonight, play all sorts of stupid things... Oh well!

VASILY. Why do you say we should be friends? We haven't had an argument. Have we?

NIKOLAY. You always make me feel like we have. You can be quite strange, you know.

VASILY. 'Strange, passing strange, pitiful, wondrous pitiful... Is my lord angry?'[7]

NIKOLAY. Whose lord?

Pause.

VASILY. When I'm alone with someone it's alright, I'm just like everyone else. But when lots of people are around I get nervous and shy and... I say weird things. But I'm a good person, better than these hypocrites anyway. And I can prove it.

NIKOLAY. I only get annoyed with you because you're always picking on me in public. But actually. I quite like you. So... I'm going to be drunk tonight! Cheers!

VASILY. Cheers!

They drink.

It's not personal, Baron. It's just that I have a hypersensitive character, like the poet Lermontov. (*Soft.*) I even look a bit like Lermontov... at least that's what people tell me... (*Takes out a perfume bottle, rubs perfume on his hands.*)

Enter ANDREY *with a book. He sits near them and reads.*

NIKOLAY. I've resigned my commission. Ta-dah! I thought and thought about it and I decided. I'm going to work...

VASILY. 'Is my lord angry? Then put out the light, and then put out the light...'[8]

NIKOLAY. I am going. To work.

IVAN *comes into the living room from the hall with* IRINA.

IVAN. And the meal was also authentic Caucasian. Onion soup to start, then, for the meat course, *chekhartma* /

VASILY. *Cheremsha* isn't meat, it's a plant like an onion.

IVAN. Excuse me, but *chekhartma* isn't an onion. It's a type of mutton roast.

VASILY. Well I'm telling you it's an onion.

IVAN. And I'm telling you it's mutton.

VASILY. And I'm telling you it's onion.

IVAN. Mutton!

VASILY. Onion!

IVAN. Oh what's the point of arguing with you. You've never been to the Caucasus and you've never eaten *chekhartma*.

VASILY. I've never eaten *cheremsha* because I hate it. It smells like garlic. And I know it smells like garlic because I have been to the Caucasus actually, I was sent there for duelling just like Lermontov and /

ANDREY. Please don't argue, please!

NIKOLAY. When are the musicians getting here!

IRINA. They said by nine /

NIKOLAY (*hugging* ANDREY *suddenly, singing*). 'My Bonnie lies over the ocean, my Bonnie lies over the sea…'

ANDREY (*singing*). 'My Bonnie lies over the ocean…'

IVAN (*singing*). 'Oh bring back my Boh-nnie to me-e!'

NIKOLAY, ANDREY *and* IVAN (*singing and dancing*). 'Bring back, oh bring back, oh bring back my Bonnie to me, to me! Bring back oh bring back, oh – (*Harmony.*) Bring. Ba-ck. My. Bonn-ee. To. Me-ee!'[9]

Laughter and applause.

NIKOLAY. More drinking! Everyone drink! Andryusha! Here's to our friendship! I'll come with you to Moscow, I'll come with you to the university and /

VASILY. Which one? There are two universities in Moscow.

ANDREY. There's only one university in Moscow.

VASILY. No, two!

ANDREY. Why not three? The more the merrier.

Laughter.

VASILY. There are two universities in Moscow!

Moans and heckling.

There are two universities in Moscow, the old university and
the new university. But if you don't want to know, if I irritate
you just by speaking, then I can shut up. In fact, I can even
fuck off!

Storms out to 'Ooooooooh!'

NIKOLAY. Whoops! (*Laughs.*) Right, let's have some fun. I'll
play, you dance. God he's a funny one that Vasily...

NIKOLAY *plays a waltz on the piano. They all dance.*
MASHA *walzes alone.*

MASHA (*sings*). 'The Baron is drunk, the Baron is drunk, the
Baron is drunk is drunk is drunk...'

Enter NATASHA.

NATASHA. Ivan Romanych!

They whisper together then she leaves. IVAN *goes to*
NIKOLAY *and whispers to him. He stops playing.*

IRINA. Don't stop!

IVAN. We've got to go.

IRINA. Go?

NIKOLAY. Yes, time to go unfortunately.

IRINA. But the musicians are coming!

ANDREY. The musicians won't be coming.

Beat.

You see, darling, Natasha says that Bobik isn't very well,
I mean, he's sick so... Look I don't know, it really doesn't
matter to me.

IRINA. Oh. 'Bobik is sick.'

MASHA. So! They're throwing us out. Well I suppose we
better get out then. (*To* IRINA.) Bobik isn't the sick one, she
is... in here! (*Taps her head.*) Suburban little woman.

Exit ANDREY *to his study,* IVAN *with him. The others leave
through the hall.*

ALEXEY. What a shame! I was looking forward to a party, but
if the baby's sick then the baby's sick. I'll bring him a little
toy in the morning...

VLADIMIR. I had a nap after lunch because I thought we'd be
dancing all night. But it's not even nine o clock!

MASHA. Let's just get out of here...

*They are gone. from outside, calls of 'Goodnight' and 'Sleep
well',* NIKOLAY *laughing.* ANFISA *and a* MAID *put out
the lamps and candles. Somewhere in the house a woman is
singing to the baby.*

Enter ANDREY *and* IVAN *in hats and coats.*

IVAN. I never got married because one day I looked up and it
turned out my whole life had already happened. And I suppose
because I was in love with your mother, who was already
married...

ANDREY. Well we shouldn't get married. We shouldn't get
married because it's boring.

IVAN. But what about loneliness... Say what you want but
loneliness is a terrible thing... Not that any of it matters in
the end of course!

ANDREY. Quickly...

IVAN. Plenty of time.

ANDREY. I'm worried Natasha will try and stop me.

IVAN. Ah ha!

ANDREY. I'm not going to play today anyway, I'm just going
to watch. I don't feel well in fact... Dear doctor, what should
I do about this... Breathlessness?

IVAN. You're asking me? I really don't know, I don't remember any more.

Doorbell. Voices, laughter outside.

ANDREY. Let's go through the kitchen...

Exit ANDREY *and* IVAN.

Another bell, more laughter.

Enter IRINA.

IRINA. Who is it?

ANFISA. The musicians!

Doorbell again.

IRINA. Tell them. Tell them we went out Nanny. Tell them we're sorry.

Exit ANFISA.

IRINA *alone.*

Enter VASILY.

VASILY. Empty... Where is everyone?

IRINA. Gone.

VASILY. Odd... So you're alone?

IRINA. Yes.

Pause.

Goodnight.

VASILY. I know I was out of control just then but. You're not like the others, you're better than them, you can see who I really am... You're the only person who understands me and I love, I'm completely in love / with

IRINA. Goodnight! Please go away.

VASILY (*following her*). I can't live without you, I'm only happy when I'm with you. There's something about your eyes, they're so expressive and beautiful it's wonderful, you're the only woman in the world with eyes like /

IRINA. Leave me alone!

Beat.

VASILY. I told you I love you. I'm not here any more. I'm somewhere else. (*Puts his hand over his eyes.*) Oh well, it doesn't matter. You can't make someone love you back. Obviously... But there can't be anyone else... There can't... Do you understand me? I'll kill I will kill anyone who /

Enter NATASHA *in a dressing gown with a candle.*

NATASHA. He's in there isn't he, reading reading... Let him read... Oh! Vasily Vasilich, I'm sorry! I didn't know you were here, I'm not dressed /

VASILY. It doesn't matter. Goodnight!

Exit VASILY.

NATASHA. Sweetie! Look at you! You're exhausted...
(*Kisses* IRINA.) You should have been in bed hours ago.

IRINA. Is Bobik asleep?

NATASHA. Yes, but he's restless. Which reminds me, I've been meaning and meaning to ask you but you're never here, or when you are I'm so busy... Bobik's nursery is, I think, too cold and damp for a baby, but your lovely little room is perfect. Darling sweetest loveliest Irina, please move in with Olga, just for a tiny little while!

IRINA. What do you mean?

Bells outside.

NATASHA. You and Olga can share a room and then Bobik can have your room. He's such a perfect little thing, today I said to him, 'Bo-bik! You're mine! All mine!' and he *looked* at me. With his eyes.

Doorbell.

That'll be Olga, finally!

The MAID *comes in and whispers to* NATASHA.

Protopopov? Really? Protopopov wants me to go for a ride with him? (*Laughs*.) Aren't these men hilarious...

Doorbell.

And there's someone else... I suppose I could go for just a teeny weeny little fifteen minutes... Tell him I'm coming.

Doorbell.

Still ringing, must be Olga, yes...

Exit NATASHA *with the* MAID.

IRINA *alone*.

Enter FYODOR, OLGA *and* ALEXANDER.

FYODOR. Strange. I thought they were having a party?

ALEXANDER. When I left half an hour ago they were waiting for the musicians...

IRINA. Everyone's gone.

FYODOR. What? Has Masha gone? Where has she gone? And why is Protopopov sitting outside in a sleigh? Who is he waiting for?

IRINA. Stop asking me questions! I'm tired...

FYODOR. Sulky...

OLGA. The meeting's only just finished. I'm exhausted. The headmistress was ill and I had to stand in for her and I've got such a headache, my head aches and aches... (*Sits*.) Andrey lost two hundred roubles yesterday... The whole town's talking...

FYODOR. Yes. (*Sits*.) I too found the meeting very tiring.

ALEXANDER. Well my wife decided to terrify me and nearly poisoned herself. Thank god everything's alright now and I can relax... But we've got to go have we? Well then, goodnight to you both. Fyodor Ilyich! Let's go somewhere together! I can't go home, I really can't... Let's go out!

FYODOR. No, I'm too tired. (*Stands.*) Too tired... Has Masha gone home?

IRINA. I guess so.

FYODOR (*kissing* IRINA *goodnight*). Well goodnight then. Tomorrow and the day after tomorrow I can sleep all day if I want to! (*Goes.*) I'd have loved some tea though. I was hoping to spend the evening here with my friends...

ALEXANDER. Fine. I guess I'll just go alone then...

They leave together.

FYODOR (*off*). *O fallacem hominum spem!* How deceitful are the hopes of men.

ALEXANDER (*off, whistles* MASHA's *song*).

FYODOR (*off*). That's the accusative case for exclamations...

They're gone.

OLGA. My head my head my head... Andrey lost again... The whole town's talking... I've got to go to bed. (*Goes.*) Tomorrow I'm free... Oh my god how wonderful! Free tomorrow, free the day after tomorrow... But my head aches my head...

Exit OLGA.

The accordion in the street. Somewhere in the house a woman is singing to the baby.

Enter NATASHA *in furs.*

NATASHA. I'll be back in half an hour. Just a tiny little ride...

Exit NATASHA.

IRINA *alone.*

IRINA. Moscow. Moscow. Moscow...

ACT THREE

Early hours of the morning. An unnatural dark. An unnatural heat.

Outside alarm bells are ringing. A fire has been burning through the night.

OLGA *and* IRINA*'s bedroom. Their beds are separated by screens.* MASHA *is curled on a sofa.*

Enter OLGA *and* ANFISA.

ANFISA. They're downstairs now, sitting on the stairs just in their pyjamas and nothing else… I told them to come up, I said 'Come upstairs, you can't stay there like that,' but they just cry and cry. 'We don't know where Daddy is, what if Daddy's been burnt?' Imagine! And outside there are more people, gathering in the yard and all half-dressed…

OLGA (*taking clothes from the wardrobe*). Here, take this grey dress… And this one… And this jacket. And this skirt too Nanny… I can't believe this is happening! They're saying the whole of Kirsanovsky Lane is on fire… Here, take this… And this. The Vershinins are completely terrified… Their house nearly burnt down. They should stay the night with us, they can't possibly go home… And Little Alex has lost everything! Everything burnt, his whole apartment…

ANFISA. Olyushka I'll have to call Ferapont, I'll never carry it all…

OLGA (*rings the bell*). No one's answering tonight…

She opens the door. Through the door, a window, through the window the sky burns red and black.

A fire engine passes. Alarms.

Can someone come here? Anyone? This is horrifying I can't bear it!

Enter FERAPONT.

Here, take these… Give this to the Kolotilin sisters, they're sitting on the stairs, and this…

FERAPONT. When the French invaded in 1812 we burned Moscow to the ground. That foxed 'em!

OLGA. Quickly quickly…

FERAPONT. Right away.

Exit FERAPONT *with clothes*.

OLGA. Nanny Nanny give it all away, we don't need anything, give it all away… I'm so tired I'm breaking… The Vershinins can't go home… The girls can sleep in the living room and Alexander Ignatich can go in with the Baron… Little Alex will have to go in with the Baron too, or in the hall… And the doctor's drunk. He's gone and got drunk and can't help anyone tonight of all nights like he's done it deliberately! And Alexander's wife will have to go in the living room with the girls /

ANFISA. Olyushka don't send me away! Please don't send me away!

OLGA. What are you talking about Nanny, no one's sending you away.

ANFISA. My dearest, my treasure, I do work, I work so hard… But when I get weak and can't work any more they'll say, 'Get out!' but where do I go? Where? Eighty years old… eighty-two…

OLGA. Sit down here and have a rest… Poor Nanny you're exhausted… Nanny! You're so pale!

Enter NATASHA.

NATASHA. They're saying we should set up an association in aid of the victims of the fire. What do you think? I think it's a very nice idea. After all, it's the duty of the privileged to help poor people. Bobik and Sofochka are fast asleep like nothing's happening, the little angels, but the house is bursting with people and there's flu in town, I'm worried they'll catch it.

OLGA. You can't see the fire from this room. It's peaceful...

NATASHA. Mm... I must look a sight. (*A mirror.*) People are saying I've put on weight... But it's just not true! It's not! Ahh, Masha's sleeping, she's all worn out... (*To* ANFISA.) What are you doing sitting down there? Get up! Get up immediately! Get out of here and make yourself useful!

Exit ANFISA.

Pause.

I just don't understand why you keep that old woman.

OLGA. I'm sorry. But I think I'm the one who doesn't understand...

NATASHA. She's old and she's useless. She should go back to her village... You're just indulging her really. I like order in the house and order in the house means no unnecessary staff. Look at you! Poor sweetie, you're tired. Our little headmistress is tired! You know, when my Sofochka grows up and goes to school I'm going to be very frightened of you.

OLGA. I'm not going to be headmistress.

NATASHA. Yes you are, they've decided.

OLGA. I'll refuse... I can't... I can't do it I... You were so rude to Nanny just now... I'm sorry but I can't allow it I... I'm going to be sick...

NATASHA (*upset*). I'm sorry Olga I didn't mean to upset you!

MASHA *gets up and walks out with a cushion.*

OLGA. Maybe we were brought up strangely, maybe we were, but you need to understand that I can't tolerate that sort of. It depresses me, it makes me feel like giving up /

NATASHA (*kisses her*). I'm sorry I'm sorry I'm sorry...

OLGA. Rudeness or cruelty or. Even shouting upsets me /

NATASHA. I know I get overexcited sometimes and say the wrong things. But even so you have to admit she should go back to her village.

OLGA. She's been with us for thirty. Years.

NATASHA. And she's too old to work now! Either I can't understand you or you're refusing to understand me. She literally isn't capable, she just sleeps and *sits* and /

OLGA. So let her sit.

Beat.

NATASHA. What do you mean let her sit? But she's *staff*! Staff don't sit! I don't understand you at all Olya. I have a nanny and a wet-nurse for the children, we have a maid, a cook... Why do we need that old woman? Tell me! Why?

Fire alarms outside.

OLGA. I've aged ten years in just one night.

NATASHA. We're going to have to come to some kind of agreement Olya. You're at school all day, I'm at home, you're the teacher, I am the housekeeper. And if I say something about the staff, then I know what I'm talking about. I. Know. What. I'm. Talk-ing. About... And I want that old thief, that old *bitch* out of this house first thing in the morning! (*Stamps.*) How dare she take advantage of me! How dare she! And now she's upset me how *dare* she!

Beat.

Yes. The thing is, if you don't move out we're always going to be arguing like this. It's terrible.

Enter FYODOR.

FYODOR. Is Masha in here? We ought to go home soon. They say the fire's dying down. Only one block was burnt out in the end but because of the wind we thought the whole town would go up. (*Sits.*) I'm exhausted... Ohh Olechka, dear Olechka... You know I sometimes think, if I hadn't married Masha then I'd marry you. You're so good... I'm exhausted. (*Stops. Listens.*)

OLGA. What?

FYODOR. It's the doctor. You'd think he'd done it on purpose, he's gone and got catastrophically drunk. (*Stands.*) He's coming this way I think… Yes, he's coming in here! (*Laughs.*) Unbelievable! I'm going to hide.

He hides behind the wardrobe.

He's *so* naughty!

OLGA. Not a drop for years and now tonight he goes and gets drunk…

Enter IVAN. NATASHA *and* OLGA *stay very still. He crosses the room steadily, as though sober. He goes to a washbasin and methodically washes his hands.*

IVAN. Fuck 'em… Fuck the lot of 'em… They think just because you're a doctor you know how to cure things but actually you know fuck-all. You've forgotten everything, everything you ever knew. You know no. Things.

OLGA *and* NATASHA *slip out.*

Fuck. Them. Last Wednesday you were called to a woman in the village and she died. And it's your fault she died. Yes… Your fault… Maybe you knew some things twenty-five years ago but now you know nothing. No. Thing… Your head is empty and your heart is cold. In fact, you might not even be a human being. Maybe you just look like a human being with arms and legs and… a head. Maybe you don't actually exist at all, maybe you just think that you walk and eat and sleep and – (*Cries.*) I don't want to exist I don't want to exist! (*Stops crying.*) Fuck it… The day before yesterday everyone in the club was talking about Shakespeare and Voltaire… You've never read Shakespeare or Voltaire have you? No you haven't, but you nodded intelligently and pretended you had and everyone else did exactly the same it's so ignorant! So humiliating! And suddenly the dead woman walked into the room and you knew that you'd murdered her… You are a deformed, polluted, hateful –

Beat.

So off the wagon you hopped straight into every bottle you could get your hands on...

Enter IRINA, ALEXANDER *and* NIKOLAY. NIKOLAY *in smart civilian clothes.*

IRINA. In here, no one will come in here...

ALEXANDER. Thank god for the soldiers! Excellent boys! The whole town would've burned down without them.

FYODOR (*coming out from behind the wardrobe*). Does anyone have the time?

NIKOLAY. Already after three. It's getting light.

IRINA. They're all still sitting downstairs in the hall, no one wants to go. And Vasily's there, he just sits and sits... Ivan, you should go to bed now.

IVAN. Thank you, I'm fine. (*Combs his beard.*)

FYODOR (*laughs*). Absolutely sozzled! Good work doctor! Very good work. *In vino veritas*, as the ancients said.

NIKOLAY. People have been asking me to organise a benefit concert for the victims.

IRINA. Oh. But who would play?

NIKOLAY. We could sort it out if we wanted to. Masha plays the piano brilliantly.

FYODOR. Yes! Wonderfully!

IRINA. Not any more, she's forgotten how. She hasn't played for at least three years.

NIKOLAY. There isn't a single person in this town who appreciates music, not really. But I do understand it and, trust me, your sister is excellent. She almost has talent.

FYODOR. You're quite right Baron. I love Masha very very much. She's an extraordinary human being.

NIKOLAY. To be able to play so well and know that no one can hear you!

FYODOR. Yes... But. Would it really be... Appropriate? For her to perform in a concert I mean.

Pause.

I don't know about these things myself. It might be alright. Of course our headmaster is a very progressive man, very open-minded, but he does have certain. Opinions... Not that it's any of his business really, but if you'd like I can have a little word with him?

IVAN picks up a porcelain clock and turns it over and over in his hands, looking at it very closely.

ALEXANDER. I'm covered in soot and filth. I'm like some inhuman creature.

Pause.

I heard yesterday that they're going to transfer our brigade. Poland maybe, or the eastern border. Somewhere far off anyway.

NIKOLAY. I heard that too... So! The town will be deserted without you.

IRINA. We're leaving soon too /

IVAN drops the clock. It smashes.

IVAN. Smithereens!

Pause. Distress.

FYODOR (*runs to pick up the pieces*). Ivan Romanych how could you be so careless with something so valuable! Zero-minus for behaviour!

IRINA. That was Mummy's clock...

IVAN. Maybe it was Mummy's clock and maybe it wasn't! Maybe I didn't break it but it just looks like I broke it and maybe it looks like we exist when actually none of us are here at all! I don't know anything, you don't know anything, no one knows anything!

He is at the door now.

What? What are you all staring at?

Beat.

Natasha's fucking Protopopov. That's right. They're having a little affair and you can't even see it. You all *sit* here *staring* and you don't see a thing and Natasha's fucking Protopopov.

Goes.

'Shall I part my hair behind? Do I dare to eat a peach…'[10]

Gone.

ALEXANDER. Yes… (*Laughs.*) It's all a bit strange, isn't it?

Pause.

The moment I heard about the fire I ran straight home, our house is safe, thank god, but then I see my two little girls. They're standing there, just standing on the doorstep in their nightdresses. And their mother's nowhere to be seen. People are running and shouting, animals let loose, horses, dogs, and the expression on my daughters' faces… Fear, horror, pleading… My heart stopped when I saw those faces. 'My god,' I thought, 'What more are they going to have to live through in their long lives?' I grab them and I run and run and all I can think over and over is 'What are they going to have to live through in this world!'

Fire alarms outside.

Pause.

I get here and their mother's in the hall. Angry. Shouting. Raving.

Enter MASHA with her cushion.

When my girls were standing barefoot in the doorway and the street was red with the fire and thick with the noise I thought this must have been what it was like years ago when our enemies invaded and swept through, killing, looting, burning and –

Anyway, things are different now. And one day they'll look back on us too with horror and disgust. The way we live now

will seem exhausting and uncomfortable, and very strange.
Life will be so beautiful then! (*Laughs.*) I'm sorry, I've
started rambling again. Do you mind if I keep talking? I feel
like I need to just keep talking right now...

Pause.

You're all asleep anyway... Here's what I believe, one day
life is going to be beautiful! And all *we* can do is dream
about it. There are only three people like you in this town
today, but soon there'll be more, more and still more, and
then everyone will think the way you think, everyone will
live the way you want to live until you too become past and
people appear who are so much better than you... (*Laughs.*)
I feel so strange today... I have a terrible longing to live...
(*Hums* MASHA*'s song.*)

MASHA (*picks it up*).

ALEXANDER (*returns it*).

MASHA (*a questioning phrase*).

ALEXANDER (*concludes it. Laughs*).[11]

Enter ALEXEY, *dancing about.*

ALEXEY. Burnt burnt! Everything burnt!

Laughter.

IRINA. That isn't funny! Little Alex have you really lost
everything?

ALEXEY (*laughs*). Everything! There's nothing left. My
guitar's burnt, my camera's burnt and all my letters: ashes!
I had a little notebook to give you and that's burnt too!

Enter VASILY.

IRINA. No go away Vasily Vasilich! You can't come in.

VASILY. Why is the Baron allowed in here but not me?

Beat.

ALEXANDER. We should all be heading off actually. How's
the fire?

VASILY. Burning out. But you know, I think it's very mysterious that the Baron's allowed in your room but I'm not. (*Rubs his hands with perfume.*)

ALEXANDER (*hums* MASHA*'s song*).

MASHA (*returns it*).

ALEXANDER (*laughs*). Come on Vasily, let's go downstairs.

VASILY. Yes sir. But I won't forget this. 'No no by the hair on my chinny chin chin!'[12]

NIKOLAY *is asleep.*

Blah blah blah!

Exit VASILY *with* ALEXANDER *and* ALEXEY.

IRINA. I can't breathe. That man has choked the room out with his perfume… The Baron's asleep! Baron! Wake up!

NIKOLAY. But I'm tired… Yes… The brick factory…

IRINA. Baron!

NIKOLAY. It's alright, I'm awake. I really was thinking about the brick factory. I'll be leaving to start work there soon, it's all confirmed… (*To* IRINA.) Oh look… You're so pale, and lovely and fascinating… You light up the dark, you're a light… But you're sad, your life is making you sad… Oh please come with me and we'll live and work together /

MASHA. Time to go Nikolay!

NIKOLAY (*laughs*). You're here! I didn't see you. Alright, I'm going… (*Kisses* IRINA *goodnight.*) You know, looking at you now I remember how once upon a time it was your birthday, you were happy and full of life, and talked about how work was the most important joyful thing in the world… I couldn't take my eyes off you and all I could think was 'Life is beautiful.' Where did it go? (*Kisses her again.*) You're crying. I'm sorry, go to bed now, it's getting light… Morning breaking… But if you'd let me I'd give you my entire life /

MASHA. Nikolay Lvovich go away! Honestly…

NIKOLAY. I'm going. I'm gone…

Exit NIKOLAY.

MASHA. Fyodor? Are you asleep?

FYODOR. Mmm?

MASHA. We should go home.

FYODOR. Masha... My Masha...

IRINA. Leave her alone Fedya, she's exhausted.

FYODOR. My wife is a good person, a wonderful... I love you, I only love you /

MASHA (*angry*). *Amo, amas, amat, amamus, amatis, amant.*

FYODOR (*laughs*). No really, she's amazing. We've been married for seven years and it seems like it was yesterday. Honestly. You are an extraordinary woman. I am happy, happy, happy!

MASHA. Well I'm bored bored bored... And I can't stop thinking about it... I have to say something it's like a nail being hammered into my head. Andrey has mortgaged the house. Andrey has mortgaged the house. Andrey has mortgaged the house he's mortgaged the house and his wife snatched all the money but it's not just his house, it belongs to all four of us! He *knows* that, he *knows* that and if he had any integrity left he'd /

FYODOR. It's not worth it Masha! What can we do? Andryusha owes money all over the place.

MASHA. No. It's outrageous.

FYODOR. We aren't poor. I work hard, I go to school all day and then in the evenings I give private lessons... I'm an ordinary hard-working person... *Omnia mea mecum porto.* Everything I need I carry with /

MASHA. It isn't about that! I don't want anything. It's the injustice of it that's killing me.

Pause.

Go home, Fyodor.

FYODOR (*kisses her*). You're tired. Have a little rest then we'll go home together. Have a little sleep... (*He goes.*) Happy happy happy...

Gone.

IRINA. Andrey's sort of become less of a human being hasn't he? He's just a husk, an ageing husk... It's that woman! Do you remember when he was going to be a professor? And yesterday he was boasting, actually boasting, about becoming a member of the Local Council. He's a *member* of the council that Protopopov is Chairman of... The whole town's laughing at him and he's the only one who doesn't know, doesn't see and then tonight everyone ran to help with the fire and he went into his study and shut the door like it wasn't happening he just plays his violin over and over it's awful awful awful! (*Cries.*) I can't take any more I can't I can't...

Enter OLGA.

Throw me away throw me away throw me away...

OLGA (*afraid.*) Darling what's happened what's wrong!

IRINA. Where did it go? Where is it I lost it oh my god oh my god everything's gone I don't remember how to say 'window' in Italian or 'ceiling' I've forgotten everything and every day I forget a little bit more and life just keeps on going on and will never come back and we'll never go to Moscow... I know we'll never go...

OLGA. My love my love my love...

IRINA. I'm so unhappy I can't even work any more I can't work I won't work I – Stop! Stop. (*Controls herself.*) First I worked at the telegraph office. Now I work at the council and I hate and despise everything they tell me to do... I'm nearly twenty-four, I've been working for years, my brain is withered, I've got thin, I've got ugly, I've got old, and I get nothing in return no fulfilment or pleasure from anything and time won't stop passing and I'm moving further and further away from a real life a beautiful life into some kind of void and I'm so unhappy

I am so unhappy! I don't understand how I'm alive at all,
I don't know why I haven't killed myself...

OLGA. Don't cry little one, please don't cry... It hurts me so
much to see you cry...

IRINA. I'm not crying, I'm not crying... Stop! There. I'm not
crying any more. Stop! Stop. (*Stops.*)

OLGA. Darling... I'm going to give you some advice as a sister,
as a friend. Irina. You should marry the Baron.

IRINA (*cries again, soft*).

OLGA. I know I *know* you're not in love with him, but he's
honest, he's a good man, you respect him and that's so
important... And people don't get married for love in real life.
At least, that's what I think. I would marry without love.
I would. If someone asked me I'd marry them in a second as
long as they were a good person. I'd even marry an old man...

IRINA. I was waiting till we moved to Moscow because
I thought I'd meet him there. I imagined him, I dreamt about
him, I've already loved him... But it's all turned out to be
nothing at all...

OLGA. Darling lovely little sister, I understand, I do. When
Nikolay left the army and came here for the first time
without his uniform he was so plain and ordinary it broke my
heart. 'Why are you crying?' he asked. What could I say!
But if he'd been your husband then I would have been happy
to see him, always happy, because that's different. It's a
different thing altogether.

NATASHA *comes into the room with a candle, crosses the
room, and goes out the other side.*

MASHA. Look at her. Walking around like she started the fire.

OLGA. You, Masha, are just. Silly. I'm sorry, but you're the
silliest person in our family.

Pause.

MASHA. I need to tell you both something. I need to tell my sisters. It's my secret but it's been killing me not saying anything... I'll tell you now and then I'll never tell anyone else. I'll never say anything ever again...

Pause.

I'm in love. I'm in love with. That man. You know which man. He was here just now... Oh what's the point. I love Alexander Ignatevich / Vershinin

OLGA (*goes behind her screen*). I don't want to know! I can't hear you anyway /

MASHA. What am I going to do? First I thought he was strange, then I felt sorry for him... Then I fell in love... I love his voice, how he talks, his sadness, I love his two little girls...

OLGA. I can't hear you! Whatever stupidities you're coming out with this time, I can't hear you!

MASHA. You're the silly one Olga! If I'm in love then I'm in love. I can't control it, I can't do anything about it. And he loves me... It's terrifying! Don't you think it's terrifying? But is it actually *wrong*? (*Holds* IRINA.) Irina we're going to get through this, somehow we're going to get through this whatever happens... When you read about love in books it just seems like some stupid cliché, but then you fall in love yourself and it's like nobody has ever been in love before and nobody knows anything about it and you're all alone... Dear sisters... So now I've told you. And now, as promised, I'll never speak about it again... I'll be like Gogol's madman... 'Never mind, never mind... Silence...'[13]

Enter ANDREY, *followed by* FERAPONT.

ANDREY. What do you want! I don't understand!

FERAPONT. I've told you and told you ten times Andrey /

ANDREY. First of all, I am not Andrey to you, but sir!

FERAPONT. The firemen, Sir Andrey, have been asking to go through the garden to the river. They've been going the long way round, it's torture /

ANDREY. Fine! Tell them it's fine.

Exit FERAPONT.

Why can't they leave me alone... Where's Olga?

OLGA *comes out from behind her screen.*

There you are. Give me the little key, for the safe, I've lost mine. I know you've got a spare.

OLGA (*gives him a key from her ring of house keys*).

IRINA *goes behind her screen.*

Pause.

ANDREY. What a huge fire! It's dying down now... Tch. Shit... Ferapont annoyed me and I was stupid about it. 'Sir Andrey.' How embarrassing...

Pause.

What?

Pause.

Okay stop looking at me like that. We're going to put an end to this right now... You're here, Masha's here, Irina's here: good. Once and for all, cards on the table, what have you all got against me. What?

OLGA. Not now Andryusha. Let's talk tomorrow. (*Upset, sudden.*) This is the worst night the worst night the worst night!

ANDREY (*embarrassed*). I didn't mean to upset you. I was asking very calmly. Just tell me why you're all angry with me?

ALEXANDER (*off, whistles* MASHA's *song*).

MASHA (*whistles it back, stands*). Goodnight Olga, you should get some sleep. (*Behind* IRINA's *screen.*) Goodnight little one, sweet dreams… Bye Andrey. Leave them alone now, they're exhausted… We can talk about it tomorrow…

Exit MASHA.

OLGA. Really Andryusha, let's talk tomorrow. (*Goes behind her screen.*) Time for bed.

ANDREY. I'll just say one thing and then I'll go… Right. Firstly, don't think I haven't noticed that you all took against my wife the moment we got married. If you want to know, Natasha is a good and honest person. She's straightforward and kind and. That's my opinion. I love and respect my wife, do you understand? I love. And respect. My wife. And I insist that others respect her too. I repeat, she is an honest person, a good person, and all your little *issues*… Well I'm sorry but it's just immature.

Pause.

Secondly, you seem to be angry that I didn't become a professor, that I didn't dedicate my life to academia like we'd planned. But I serve our country, I am now, in fact, a member of our Local Council, and I consider this service to be just as vital and important as services to art and science. I am a member of the Local Council and I'm proud of it. So there.

Pause.

Finally… I have something to say… I mortgaged the house without your permission… I was wrong to do that and I'm asking you to forgive me. But I had debts I… Thirty-five thousand… I've stopped gambling, I gave up a long time ago, but actually, in my defence, you're girls, you get an annuity from our father's pension whereas money doesn't just land in my –

Pause.

Enter FYODOR.

FYODOR. Where's Masha? Isn't she in here? Strange…

Exit FYODOR.

ANDREY. They're not listening… Natasha is a good and honest person –

He paces. Then stops.

When I got married I really thought we were all going to be happy, all of us together… But… (*Cries.*) Don't believe me don't believe me don't believe me…

Exit ANDREY.

Empty stage.

FYODOR (*in the doorway*). Is Masha really not in here? But where has she gone? How bizarre! (*Gone.*)

Empty stage.

The fire alarms outside.

Knocking from below.

IRINA (*behind her screen*). Olya?

OLGA (*behind her screen*). Yes.

IRINA (*behind her screen*). Who's knocking?

OLGA (*behind her screen*). It's Ivan. He's drunk.

IRINA (*behind her screen*). Oh. It's like a nightmare.

Pause.

(*Behind her screen.*) Olya!

OLGA (*behind her screen*). Yes.

IRINA (*pokes her head out*). Did you hear? They're taking the brigade away from us, they're going to send them far away.

OLGA (*behind her screen*). It's just a rumour.

IRINA. But we're going to be all alone… (*Goes back behind her screen.*)

Beat.

(*Pokes her head out again.*) Olya!

OLGA (*behind her screen*). What!

IRINA. You're right, I do respect the Baron. He is a good man and I'll marry him, I promise I will, but please can we all go to Moscow! I'm begging you now, let's go! There's nowhere in the world that's better than Moscow! Let's go Olya, let's just go!

ACT FOUR

Late morning. Autumn. Warm. Bright.

The Prozorovs' garden. An avenue of fir trees, beyond the fir trees a river, beyond the river, a wood. Table and chairs, champagne. Passers-by and soldiers from time to time around the house.

IVAN, *with army cap and stick, strangely euphoric, reads a magazine.* IRINA, FYODOR, *with a medal but without a moustache, and* NIKOLAY *are saying goodbye to* ALEXEY *and* VLADIMIR. *Both officers are in marching uniform.*

NIKOLAY (*kisses* ALEXEY). We've had such good times together! (*Kisses* VLADIMIR.) And again, goodbye.

IRINA. Goodbye!

ALEXEY. Goodbye forever!

FYODOR. Don't say that! I'll start crying.

IRINA. We'll meet again won't we?

ALEXEY. Well, maybe in ten or fifteen years? But then we'll barely recognise each other and we'll be cold and shy... Now stay still... Just one last time...

A photograph: IRINA, FYODOR *and* NIKOLAY.

VLADIMIR (*hugs* NIKOLAY). This is it... (*Kisses* IRINA.) Thank you for everything, everything!

ALEXEY. I said stay still!

A photograph: with VLADIMIR.

NIKOLAY. I'm sure we'll see each other again. Write to us, don't forget to write!

VLADIMIR. Goodbye trees! (*Shouts.*) Echo!

ECHO. Echo…

Pause.

VLADIMIR. Goodbye echo!

FYODOR. Maybe you'll find a wife out there in Poland…
A nice little wife to hold you close and say 'My love!'
(*Laughs.*)

ALEXEY. Half an hour left… Vasily's going downriver on the
barge, but the rest of us are marching. Three batteries today,
three tomorrow – and finally peace and quiet will descend on
the town.

NIKOLAY. And everyone will die of boredom.

VLADIMIR. Where's Masha?

FYODOR. In the garden.

ALEXEY. We have to say goodbye to her.

VLADIMIR. We really need to go or I'll burst into tears.
(*Hugs* NIKOLAY *and* FYODOR, *kisses* IRINA.) We've
been so happy here…

ALEXEY (*to* FYODOR). Something to remember me by…
A notebook, and look, a tiny pencil… Down to the river
now…

They go.

VLADIMIR. Echo!

ECHO. Echo…

FYODOR. Goodbye!

They meet MASHA *coming in, and run off with her.*

IRINA. They're gone…

IVAN. They forgot to say goodbye to me!

IRINA. Well what about you?

IVAN. That's true. I forgot too somehow. I'll be seeing them soon
anyway, I'm off tomorrow. Yes… Just one little day left…

Then in a year they'll retire me and I'll come back and live out
my days with you… Just one year until my pension…
(*Swaps magazines*.) I'll come back here and radically change
my lifestyle. I'll be very quiet and… Well-behaved. Butter
wouldn't melt, you'll see…

IRINA. You really do need to change, my love. You really do.

IVAN. Yes. I know. (*Sings*.) 'Ta ra ra… Boom dee ay, I drank
my life away…'[14]

FYODOR. Nothing to be done! He's a lost cause!

IVAN. It's true. I am. If you'd been my teacher I'd have set
myself straight.

IRINA. Fyodor's shaved his moustache off. I can't look at him!

FYODOR. Why?

IVAN. I *could* tell you what your face looks like now, but I won't.

FYODOR. But this is the fashion these days, the *modus vivendi*.
Our headmaster is clean-shaven and as soon as I was made
deputy I shaved mine off. Nobody likes it, but that doesn't
matter. I'm happy. With a moustache, without a moustache,
I am equally happy. (*Sits*.)

Enter ANDREY, *wheeling a pram*.

IRINA. Ivan Romanych my love, my darling, I'm feeling really
anxious today… You were in town last night weren't you?
What happened?

IVAN. What happened? Nothing. Silly nonsense. (*Reads his
magazine*.) It doesn't matter.

FYODOR. I heard that Vasily and the Baron bumped into each
other outside the /

NIKOLAY. Oh shut up!

Exit NIKOLAY, *into the house*.

FYODOR. Outside the theatre… Vasily started getting at him,
you now how he does, and so the Baron /

IVAN. I don't know anything about it. It's all just silly silly nonsense.

FYODOR. Earlier this week I returned a boy's essay with the comment 'Nonsense' and he spent all day puzzling over it because he thought I'd written in Latin! (*Laughs*.) Absolutely hilarious![15]

Beat.

Vasily's in love with you so now of course he hates the Baron... Well why wouldn't he be? You're a lovely young lady. You sometimes remind me of Masha, in fact, always in your own world... Only Irina is kinder... Not, of course, that Masha isn't kind! I love her. Masha.

VOICE (*off*). Hello-o!

ECHO. Hello...

IRINA. Everything's making me jump today...

Pause.

I'm all packed and ready to go, they're collecting my things after dinner. Tomorrow Nikolay and I are getting married, tomorrow we're going straight to the brick factory, and the day after tomorrow I'm going to be a teacher with a whole new life to live! When I passed the exams I was so happy I actually cried...

Pause.

They're coming for my things after dinner...

FYODOR. I know you're excited Irina, but actually this is all not very realistic. It's just the same old fantasies you've always –

But I wish you the best. With all my heart.

IVAN. Little bird... You've gone so far away from me, you've gone where I can't follow... I'm too old to fly now and I've been left behind. But you keep flying, my darling, fly on!

Pause.

I'll tell you what your face looks like now Fyodor, it looks like an arse.

FYODOR. Right that's enough! (*Sighs.*) So the army is leaving and everything will go back to normal. Whatever people say, Masha is a good person, an honest person. I love her very much and I'm grateful every day that I married her. Fate's a funny thing isn't it... There's a man, Kozyrev, who's a cleaner in the council offices. We were at school together but he got expelled in the fifth year because he couldn't get his head around the *ut consecutivum*. Now he's poor, he's sick, and whenever I meet him in the street I say, 'Hello *ut consecutivum*!' And he says, *'Ut consecutivum*, that's the one.' And then he coughs... But I've been lucky all my life, I'm happy, I've been awarded a medal for services to education, and now I myself teach others the *ut consecutivum*. Of course I'm clever, cleverer than most, but that's not what makes you happy, in the end...

Inside the house someone, presumably NATASHA, *plays 'The Maiden's Prayer' on the piano. They all die inside.*

IRINA. This time tomorrow I'll never have to listen to that *bloody 'Maiden's Prayer'* ever again! And I won't have to see that Protopopov ever again either...

Pause.

He's sitting in there now. In our living room. Today of all days...

FYODOR. Is our headmistress here yet?

MASHA *walks past and away again.*

IRINA. No. We've called her. I can't tell you how hard it's been living here without Olya... Now she's headmistress she lives at the school, she's always busy and I'm all alone, I'm bored, I've got nothing to do, and the room that woman put me in is horrible... So I decided: If I'm not going to make it to Moscow, fine. That's life. Nothing to be done... And then Nikolay proposed... He's a good man. It's amazing, in fact, how good he is... I thought about it, I made a choice and suddenly I felt like I'd grown wings, my unhappiness lifted with them, everything seemed possible again and again I was seized with a longing to work and work and... But yesterday something happened and no one will tell me /

IVAN. *Nonsera nonserum nonseribus*: nonsense.[16]

NATASHA (*in the window*). Our headmistress has arrived!

FYODOR. Oh good! Let's go and say hello.

Exit FYODOR *with* IRINA.

IVAN (*reads his magazine, sings*). 'Ta ra ra... Boom dee ay... I drank my life away...'

ANDREY *pushes his pram.*

Enter MASHA.

MASHA. Here he is. Having a little sit-down.

IVAN. Well why not?

MASHA. Why not indeed... (*Sits with him.*)

Pause.

Ivan.

IVAN. Yes?

MASHA. Did you love my mother?

IVAN. Very much.

MASHA. Did she love you?

IVAN (*after some thought*). That... I can't remember any more.

MASHA. Is my man here? That's what our cook Marfa used to call her policeman. My man. Is my man here?

IVAN. Not yet.

MASHA. When you have to snatch at happiness in bits and pieces like I have, then lose it all again like I have, you become hard and angry. Like I have... (*Puts her hand to her chest.*) There's something inside me spilling over, something right here, seething... (*Looks at* ANDREY.) There goes our talented precocious brother Andrey... All our hopes and dreams. Thousands of people came together to raise a great church bell, so much work and so much money went into it and suddenly, without explanation, it fell and shattered into dust. Suddenly, for no reason at all. Andrey...

ANDREY. It's so noisy in the house! When will they all go away?

IVAN. Soon. (*Takes out a pocket watch and winds it.*) I have this old watch, you have to wind it but it chimes so prettily...

The watch chimes twelve.

The first, second and fifth batteries are leaving at twelve-thirty on the dot.

Pause.

And I'm going tomorrow.

ANDREY. Will you come back?

IVAN. Maybe. Next year when I'm retired... Well fuck. Who knows? It doesn't matter anyway...

Somewhere, far away, a violin and harp are playing.

ANDREY. The town's going to be deserted. Like someone blew a candle out. Poof!

Pause.

Something happened yesterday outside the theatre. Everyone's talking about it but of course no one tells me anything.

IVAN. It's nothing. Silly silly nonsense. Vasily was teasing the Baron, the Baron finally cracked and insulted Vasily, so Vasily decides he has to challenge the Baron to a duel. (*Checks his watch.*) Now, in fact... At midday, in the woods over the river... Bang bang! (*Laughs.*) Vasily thinks he's Lermontov or something, he's even started writing poetry. Well of course we all laugh at him but the fact of the matter is, it's his third duel.

MASHA. Whose?

IVAN. Vasily's.

MASHA. And the Baron?

IVAN. What about the Baron?

Pause.

MASHA. Everything just went dark… I don't think it should be allowed. He could hurt Nikolay, kill him even.

IVAN. The Baron's a very nice baron, but one baron more, one Baron less, does it really matter in the end? No it does not, so let them get on with it!

VOICE (*off*). Hello-o!

ECHO. Hello…

IVAN. You can just wait. That's the second calling me. He's in the boat already.

Pause.

ANDREY. Well in my opinion taking part in a duel, even as a doctor, is just wrong.

IVAN. It might seem like that but… Actually there is nothing at all in the whole world. We aren't really here, we don't exist, it just seems like we do… And it doesn't matter does it.

MASHA. There they go! All day long, talk talk talk… (*Goes.*) First you have to live in this bloody place, it could randomly start snowing any second now, and then they have to have these absurd conversations and – (*Stops.*) No. I'm not going into that house. I can't go in there… When Alexander comes will you call me… (*Goes down the fir tree avenue.*) Oh look, look up!

They all look up.

The birds are migrating… Swans. No. Geese… Lovely happy birds…

Exit MASHA.

ANDREY. Our house is going to be empty. The officers are leaving, you're leaving, my little sister's getting married. I'm going to be all alone.

IVAN. What about your wife?

Enter FERAPONT *with papers*.

ANDREY. My wife is my wife. She is honest and kind and, well, a good person. And yet. Sometimes I feel like there's something inside her which reduces her to the level of a blind, scaled little animal. Like she's not really human. I'm telling you this because you're my friend, you've known me since I was a boy and you're the only person I can trust. I love Natasha, it's true, I do, but sometimes she's so frighteningly small-minded I get lost, I don't understand why I love her, I don't remember why I love her. Or, at least, used to love her…

IVAN (*stands*). Tomorrow, my dear, I'm going away. We'll probably never see each other again so I'm going to give you some advice, for what it's worth. Put on your hat, take your stick, and walk out that door… Walk out that door and don't you ever look back. And the further you go, the better.

Enter VASILY *with two* OFFICERS. *The* OFFICERS *walk on*.

VASILY. There you are! It's time.

IVAN. I'm coming I'm coming. I'm sick of the lot of you. (*To* ANDREY.) If anyone asks for me just tell them I'll be back soon…

VASILY. 'Little pig little pig let me come in, no no'[17] /

IVAN (*a moan, a sigh, something pained*).

VASILY. What are you groaning about old man?

IVAN. Nothing.

VASILY. How's the health?

IVAN. Delightful!

VASILY. No need to get upset now. I'm just going to teach him a little lesson, clip his wings as such. The shoulder, perhaps…

(*Rubs perfume on his hands.*) I've already used up a whole bottle today and they still smell. They smell like rotting flesh.

Pause.

Yes…

They go.

Do you know that poem by Lermontov? 'And he, rebellious, seeks the storm, As though the storm can offer calm' /

IVAN. And it huffed and it puffed and it blew him to bits.[18]

They're gone.

VOICE. Hello-o!

ECHO. Hello…

ANDREY *wheels the pram.*

FERAPONT (*approaching*). Sir Andrey, some papers for you /

ANDREY. Leave me alone! Why oh why won't you leave me alone!

Exit ANDREY with pram.

FERAPONT. But papers have to be signed! It's what they're for!

Exit FERAPONT after ANDREY.

Enter IRINA and NIKOLAY. FYODOR passes.

FYODOR. Masha? Hello-o Masha?

Exit FYODOR.

NIKOLAY. There goes the only man in town who's happy the military are leaving.

IRINA. Can you blame him?

Pause.

It's going to be so empty now.

NIKOLAY. Darling, I've got to go but I'll be back soon.

IRINA. Where are you going?

NIKOLAY. Just into town, say goodbye to my friends…

IRINA. You're lying. Nikolay, what's wrong with you today?

Pause.

What happened yesterday outside the theatre?

NIKOLAY. I'll be back in an hour or so and we'll be together again. (*Kisses her.*) My love… (*Holds her face and looks at her face.*) I fell in love with you five years ago and I still can't get used to it. You're more beautiful every day. Look at your wonderful hair! Look at your wonderful eyes! Tomorrow we're going to go away, we're going to work like we always said we would, we're going to be rich, and all of my dreams are going to come true and you're going to be happy… There's just one problem. Just a little one. You don't love me.

IRINA. I can't help it. I'll marry you, I'll be your wife, I'll be faithful but I don't love you and there's nothing I can do. I've never loved anyone and I wanted to so much, I really wanted to… But it's like my heart is an expensive grand piano and they locked it up and lost the key.

Pause.

Your eyes have gone strange…

NIKOLAY. I didn't sleep all night. I'm not afraid of anything, not anything in the world. But that little lost key tortures me and won't let me sleep… Say something to me.

Pause.

Say something to me…

IRINA. What should I say? Everything's so incomprehensible. Look at the old trees standing there. They won't tell us anything… (*Lays her head on his chest.*)

NIKOLAY. Say something to me.

IRINA. What? What can I possibly say?

NIKOLAY. You know what.

IRINA. Stop! Please stop.

Pause.

NIKOLAY. Funny how sometimes small things suddenly seem
so significant. You laugh about them, just like you used to,
say they're insignificant, just like you used to, and then you
keep on going on because you aren't strong enough to stop…
Oh why are we talking about this! I'm actually feeling kind
of ecstatic. Like I'm seeing those trees clearly for the first
time, clearly seeing those firs those maples those birches.
And they're seeing me too, watching me curiously and
waiting to see what I'll do next. What beautiful trees. With
such beautiful trees to keep us company life should be
beautiful too.

VOICE. Hello-o!

ECHO. Hello…

NIKOLAY. I have to go now… That one's all dried up and
withered, but it's swaying in the wind with the others. If I die
I think I'll still be part of life somehow, just like that. Bye
bye darling… (*Kisses her.*) The papers are all on the desk in
my room, by the calendar /

IRINA. I'm coming with you.

NIKOLAY. No! No no. (*Goes. Stops.*) Irina!

IRINA. Yes!

Beat.

NIKOLAY. I didn't have any coffee this morning. Will you tell
them to make some for when I get back?

Exit NIKOLAY.

IRINA *alone.*

Enter ANDREY *pursued by* FERAPONT.

FERAPONT. I swear these aren't my papers, they're official,
I didn't make them up /

ANDREY. Where is it? Where? Where did my past go? I was young and happy and clever, my thoughts were young and happy and clever thoughts and my present and future glowed in the dark. Why when we have only just started to live do we become boring, grey, uninteresting, lazy, indifferent, useless, miserable… This town has existed for two hundred years, it has a population of one hundred thousand and there's not a single person who isn't exactly the same as everyone else, not a single original thinker, not now, not ever, not a single intellectual, a single artist, not one person who's even the tiniest bit special, who could inspire envy or a longing to be a better human being. All we do is eat, drink, sleep and die… Then other people are born and they eat, drink, sleep and, to try and make their meaningless lives bearable, they gossip and drink and gamble and sue each other over stupid things and the wives cheat on their husbands and the husbands pretend they see nothing and hear nothing and the children are crushed under the weight of all this ignorance and pettiness and any slight glimmer of a chance they might have had is put out before they've even really drawn breath and then they become the same pathetic corpses that their mothers and fathers –

Beat.

(*To* FERAPONT.) What!?

FERAPONT. You what? (*Holds out the papers.*) Papers. To be signed.

ANDREY. You're going to be the end of me. (*Takes the papers.*)

FERAPONT. The porter at the office was saying it was minus-twenty degrees in St Petersburg last winter.

ANDREY. The present is impossible. But when I imagine the future it's beautiful! Expanding effortless and uncomplicated in front of me, and far in the distance I see the dawn breaking, I see freedom, I see how my children and I will be free from apathy, from drinking, from Sunday roasts and afternoon naps, free from this parasitical relationship with the world…

FERAPONT. Two thousand people froze to death he said. People were terrified, he said. He said they declared a state of emergency. In Petersburg. Or was it Moscow? Don't remember.

ANDREY (*tender*). My sisters… My dear sisters, my wonderful sisters… (*Cries.*) Masha, my sister…

NATASHA (*at the window*). What's going on out here? Is that you Andryusha? You'll wake Sofochka. *Il ne faut pas faire du bruit, la Sophie est dormée deja. Vous etes un ours!* (*Shouts.*) If you want to shout then give the baby to someone else! Ferapont! Take the pram from Mr Prozorov!

FERAPONT. Yes madam. (*Takes the pram.*)

ANDREY. I wasn't shouting…

NATASHA (*in the window*). Boh-bik! Good Bobik, very very good OW! No bad Bobik! Very very very bad Bobik!

ANDREY. I'll take a look at these and sign what needs to be signed. If you wait then you can bring them back to the office today.

Exit ANDREY *with papers.* FERAPONT *follows, wheeling the pram.*

NATASHA (*in the window*). Boh-bik! What's your mummy's name? What's my name my little pumpkin? And look! Who's this! It's Auntie *Oll*-yah! Say 'Hello Auntie Olya!'

Two BUSKERS *come in and play the violin and the harp.* ALEXANDER, OLGA *and* ANFISA *come out of the house and listen.* IRINA *joins them.*

OLGA. Our garden's like a public park. Everyone just wanders through… Nanny, give them something will you?

ANFISA (*gives money to the* BUSKERS). There you are dear ones, thank you, off you go now…

The BUSKERS *bow and leave.*

Poor things. You don't have to play like that when you've got enough food to eat do you? (*To* IRINA.) Irinka! My littlest one! (*Hugs her.*) What a life, what a life! Fate has been kind to me in my old age. I've never, not since the day I was born, lived like this... A big apartment with our Olyushka at the school, all official and rent-free, my whole own room and my whole own bed! I wake up in the middle of the night I'm so happy, there's no one in the world who's happier than me!

ALEXANDER. We'll be leaving soon, Olga. It's time for me to go.

Pause.

I wish you all the best, all of you, I... Where's Masha?

IRINA. She was in the garden. I'll go and find her.

ALEXANDER. Would you? It's just that I don't have much time...

ANFISA. I'll go and look too.

IRINA *and* ANFISA *leave.*

Mashenka! Hello-oo!

ECHO. Hello...

ANFISA. Hello-oo Mashenka!

ECHO. Mashenka...

They're gone.

ALEXANDER. All good things come to an end, and now we have to say goodbye. (*Checks his watch.*) The town threw a sort of leaving party, lunch and champagne, the Mayor gave a speech. I ate and drank and listened, but my heart was here... I've got used to being with you.

OLGA. Will we see each other again some time?

ALEXANDER. Probably. Not.

Pause.

My wife and daughters are staying on for another month or so. If anything happens, if they need anything /

OLGA. Of course! Of course. I'll look after them, I promise.

Pause.

Funny to think that there won't be a single soldier in town tomorrow. All this will be a memory and we'll have to find a new way to live.

Pause.

Nothing happens the way you want it to happen. I didn't want to be headmistress, and here I am being headmistress. And now I'll never get back to Moscow…

ALEXANDER. Well… I want to thank you for everything. I want to say. If anything was not. I mean will you forgive me if I –

Too much. And I've already said so much. Forgive me for that too, don't think badly of me.

OLGA (*wipes her eyes*). Why isn't Masha coming!

ALEXANDER. What else can I say except goodbye? There must be some little speech I can make… (*Laughs.*) Okay. Here it is. Life is hard. It's incomprehensible and it seems hopeless. But we have to admit that it's slowly becoming more lucid and light and one day soon it will be bright as cold clear water. (*Checks his watch.*) I have to go! In the past humanity was committed to violence. We spent our time waging wars, filling the world up with campaigns, invasions, occupations, but that's all over now, leaving behind a great empty space. We don't know what we're going to fill it with yet, but we are desperately seeking what to fill that empty space with and, in the end, we'll find it… I just wish we could find it now!

Pause.

But you know, if work and education, education and work could somehow be made to… (*Checks his watch.*) I have to go /

OLGA. She's here!

Enter MASHA. OLGA moves away.

ALEXANDER. I've come to say goodbye…

MASHA. Bye then.

They kiss. A long time.

OLGA. That's enough, that's enough now…

MASHA (*cries*).

ALEXANDER. Write to me… Don't forget me! You have to let go now… I have to… Olga Sergeyevna help me! I have to go… I have to go…

He shakes OLGA*'s hands, then kisses them. He embraces* MASHA *again.*

He goes.

He's gone.

OLGA. That's enough Masha! Darling please…

Enter FYODOR.

FYODOR. Never mind never mind, she needs to cry so let her cry… Dear Masha, my good sweet Masha… You're my wife and whatever happens I'm happy… I don't mind, I don't blame you for anything… Olya is my witness… We'll start to live again just like we used to, just like we used to be and I won't say a word, not a single word…

MASHA (*sings*). 'On a curved white shore grows a green oak tree… a golden chain wound round and round…' I'm losing my mind… 'By the sea… A green tree…'

OLGA. Stop crying Masha, you have to stop crying… Give her some water!

MASHA. I'm not crying. I'm not crying…

FYODOR. She's not crying… She's a good girl…

Far away, a gunshot.

MASHA. 'On a curved white shore a golden chain… a golden chain…' I can't remember the words… A golden chain… (*Drinks water.*) My life is a failure… I don't need anything any more… I'll calm right down… It doesn't matter…

What do you think the 'curved shore' means? Why is this song stuck in my head? I don't remember the words any more...

Enter IRINA.

OLGA. Please calm down Masha. There, good girl good girl... Let's go inside /

MASHA. I'm not going into that house! (*Cries then stops immediately.*) I haven't been into that house for a long time, and I won't ever go into that house again...

IRINA. Can we all just be together for a bit? We don't have to talk or anything. It's just. I *am* leaving tomorrow...

Pause.

FYODOR. Yesterday I confiscated a false moustache and beard off a boy in the third form... (*Puts on a false moustache and beard.*) It's just like our German teacher isn't it... (*Laughs.*) Don't you think? Those boys are funny.

MASHA. You do look like the German teacher.

OLGA (*laughs*). You really do!

MASHA (*cries*).

IRINA. Please Masha!

FYODOR. Just like the German teacher...

Enter NATASHA *and a* MAID.

NATASHA. Mr Protopopov can look after Sofochka for a bit and Andrey Sergeyich can give Bobik a turn in the pram. These children are such a handful! (*To* IRINA.) Oh Irina! You're abandoning us tomorrow! It's so sad. Won't you stay just one tiny little week more?

She sees FYODOR *and screams. He takes off the false moustache and beard, laughing.*

God you gave me a fright! (*To* IRINA.) I'm so used to having you around, I hope you don't think it'll be easy for me without you? I'll get them to move Andrey and his violin into your room, he can scrape away in there as much as he likes. Then we can put Sofochka in his study. She's such a special child! And just so sweet! Today she looked at me with her little eyes and, you won't believe it: 'Ma-ma'!

FYODOR. She's a very good baby.

NATASHA. So! I'm going to be all on my own here. (*Sighs.*) First off I'll have those fir trees cut down, and that maple. They're so gloomy in the evenings it's horrible... Irina sweetie, that belt doesn't suit you at all... You need something brighter to liven you up. Then I'll have flowers planted all around the house. Hundreds of flowers! There'll be such a gorgeous smell... Why is there a fork on the bench?

Beat.

Goes into the house after the MAID.

(*Off.*) I said why is there a fork on the bench there! (*Shouts.*) Don't answer back!

FYODOR. And she's off!

The military band play a march.

OLGA. They're going.

Enter IVAN.

MASHA. Our soldiers are going. Well... Good luck to them. (*To* FYODOR.) We should go home... Where's my hat and coat?

FYODOR. I took them inside... I'll go and get them.

Exit FYODOR.

OLGA. Time for us all to go home.

IVAN. Olga Sergeyevna!

OLGA. Yes?

Pause.

What?

IVAN. Nothing… I don't really know how to tell you this…
(*Whispers to her.*)

OLGA. No!

IVAN. Yes… What a mess… I'm exhausted, drained, I don't
want to say anything ever again. (*Annoyed.*) And still I'm
telling you it doesn't matter!

MASHA. What's happened?

OLGA. Something terrible…

IRINA. What?

OLGA. I don't know what to say to you, Irina /

IRINA. Just tell me for god's sake! (*Cries.*)

IVAN. The Baron has been killed in a duel.

IRINA. I know… I know I know…

IVAN. Drained… (*Takes out a magazine.*) Let them have their
little cry… (*Sings soft.*) 'Ta ra ra boom… dee ay… I drank
my life away…' What can it possibly matter…

The three sisters are together.

MASHA. Listen to the band playing! They're leaving us now…
One of them has left us forever. And we have to stay behind
so we can try and live our lives again. We have to live… We
have to live… Look up… The geese are migrating. They
don't know why but every spring and every autumn for
thousands of years they've been flying and they'll fly for
thousands of years more until finally, all of life's mystery is
revealed to them…

IRINA. One day people will understand everything, what the
meaning of all this is, what the meaning of all this suffering
is, but for now we just have to keep living… We have to
work, we have to work! I'll leave tomorrow, I'll go on my
own and I'll take up my job in the school and give my life to
people who might just need it. It's autumn now, then it will
be winter and the earth will be covered in snow. And I'm
going to work, I am going to work…

OLGA. The music is so brave it makes you happy to be alive! Oh my god, time passes and we'll be gone forever, our faces forgotten, our voices forgotten, even how many of us were here, forgotten, but all of our suffering will transform into joy for the people who come after us. Happiness and peace will fill the world and then they'll look back and remember us kindly, the sad people who lived and died before them. My dear sisters, our lives aren't over yet. We are going to live! The music is so brave, the music is so happy and, it seems, in just a little while we'll know why we're here, and what all of this suffering is for… It is possible to know, it is possible to know!

The music gets further away.

Enter FYODOR, *smiling, with* MASHA's *hat and coat.*

ANDREY *wheels Bobik in the pram.*

IVAN (*sings soft*). 'And now I hide away, and dream of yesterday…' (*Reads his magazine.*) Doesn't matter. Doesn't matter at all…

OLGA. It is possible to know. It is possible. To know.

End.

Appendix

Chekhov's original quotations, all from Helen Rappaport's literal translation, are provided here with explanations for my adaptations.

1. *Three Sisters* is a very musical play, both in the live singing and performance, and in its finely tuned sound world. I chose to expand on this musicality by turning Masha's poetry recitation (see note 2) into a song which recurs as a love theme throughout the play. The melody for the premiere production directed by Rebecca Frecknall at the Almeida Theatre was written by Angus MacRae.

On a Curved White Shore

Words by Alexander Pushkin
Trans. Cordelia Lynn

Music by Angus MacRae

© Angus MacRae, published by Manners McDade Music Publishing

2. 'By the curved shore, a green oak tree, a golden chain around its trunk… A golden chain around its trunk…'

The opening lines of the prologue to Alexander Pushkin's narrative poem *Ruslan and Lyudmila*. These lines and the romance and folk mystery they suggest would be immediately recognisable with profound effect to a Russian audience. I felt making a song out of them would heighten a moment that could otherwise be lost on a Western audience.

3. 'He had no time to cry out "Oh!" before the bear sat on him.'

From Ivan Krylov's fable 'The Peasant and the Workman'. I wanted to find an alternative that would suggest impending disaster and violence, both in the story between Vasily and Nikolay, and for the Prozorov family. It had to be folky in nature. Rebecca suggested 'The Three Little Pigs' after we spoke about themes of homes/worlds being destroyed by outsiders. The cry of an outsider wanting to be 'let in' sits nicely with Vasily's character.

4. 'For love alone nature brought us onto this earth.'

From the French opera-vaudeville *The Werewolves*. This had to be a childish teasing of someone in love. It is repeated by Ivan over the lunch, just as the playground chant is in this version.

5. I have offered spoken translations of all of Fyodor's Latin quotations.

6. In the original it is Irina's saint or name day rather than her birthday. I wanted to convey the significance of the celebration, and also am always happy to have more singing…

7. 'I am strange, but who is not strange! Do not get angry, Aleko.'

Vasily is linking, and misquoting, two texts here. 'I am strange' is from the play *Woe from Wit* by Alexander Griboyedev. Its disaffected hero Chatsky is a Russian Hamlet equivalent. 'Don't be angry, Aleko' refers to Pushkin's poem *The Gypsies*, in which the jealous protagonist Aleko murders his mistress and her lover. Both sources are classic Russian pieces so I went with Shakespeare. I felt themes of jealousy, suspicion between friends and love-triangle disaster were the most important ones to signpost, so have used *Othello*.

8. 'Do not get angry, Aleko... Forget, forget those dreams of yours...'

Continuing from *The Gypsies*, but misquoted. I continue with *Othello*, also slightly misquoted.

9. NIKOLAY. Oh my porch, my porch, my new porch

ANDREY. My new porch of maple wood

IVAN. All latticed.

From 'Ah Vy, Seni, Moi Seni', a folk song about a young woman whose father won't let her see the man she loves. I wanted to translate the idea of lovers separated, repetition and simplicity of language, and the folk-song tone.

10. 'Would you care to take this date?'

From an operetta. Chekhov couldn't remember which when asked. I've used T.S. Eliot's *The Love Song of J. Alfred Prufrock*. The semantic similarities are clear, but the texts convey different meanings. The sexual implication is carried in both, but the operetta says something about the more playful and idle side of Ivan's character, in keeping with his quote from *The Werewolves* in Act One. I preferred to explore the deeper and sadder side to him here, his unresolved love of the Prozorovs' mother, his sense of ageing. He seems a very Prufrockian character to me. At best it's a heightened symbolic choice, at worst a dreadful cheat as *Prufrock* wasn't published till 1915, eleven years after Chekhov's death.

11. ALEXANDER (*sings*). 'All ages must submit to love, to her charitable passions!'

MASHA. Tram-tam-tam...

ALEXANDER. Tram-tam...

MASHA. Tra-ra-ra?

ALEXANDER. Tra-ta-ta. (*Laughs.*)

The quote is from Prince Gremin's love aria in Pyotr Ilyich Tchaikovsky's opera *Eugene Onegin*, after Pushkin's narrative poem. The ensuing exchange is a bit mysterious. Michael Frayn attributes it to an event from Chekhov's own life. I decided to use it to expand on Masha's song, shared between her and Alexander here almost like a code.

12. 'The moral of this I could explain at length, but I am afraid of provoking the geese.'

From 'The Geese', another Krylov fable. I chose to repeat 'The Three Little Pigs' reference as it worked well within the line.

13. 'Now I will be like Gogol's madman... Silence... Silence...'

From Nikolai Gogol's *Diary of a Madman*. I've kept all of Masha's references to Gogol as they seem clear enough. Here I expanded the quotation to include 'Never mind...' which recurs as a refrain in the Gogol, and I liked how it mirrors the *Three Sisters* refrain: 'It doesn't matter.'

14. 'Ta-ra-ra... Boom-bi-ya, I'm sitting on a kerbstone-i-ya.'

From the popular American music-hall song, which repeats 'Tarara Boomdeeay' for its chorus. Ivan is singing the standard Russian version of the song which goes, rather marvellously, 'Tarara Boombiya / I sit on a kerbstone / And I weep bitterly / That I'm of little significance.' Obviously this doesn't rhyme in English so I wrote my own version, again drawing it back to Ivan's character: 'Tarara Boomdeeay / I drank my life away / And now I hide away / And dream of yesterday.'

15. 'In some seminary or other, a teacher wrote "silly nonsense" on a pupil's essay, and the pupil read it as "renyxa" and thought he had written in Latin.'

This pun requires a working knowledge of the Cyrillic and Latin alphabets, as well as printed and handwritten Russian scripts. I turned it into a personal memory of Fyodor's, still in his Latin safe space, but the pun is lost.

16. 'Renyxa. Nonsense.'

Here Ivan refers back to Fyodor's renyxa pun, so I referred back to my replacement by writing a fake declension of 'Nonsense', Ivan's spin on the pupil's confusion over the word.

17. 'He barely had time to cry out "oh", before the bear sat on him.'

Replaced with 'The Three Little Pigs' again.

18. VASILY. Do you know remember those verses? 'And he rebellious seeks the storm / As though in storms there is peace.

IVAN. Yes. 'He barely had time to cry out "oh", before the bear sat on him.'

Vasily quotes from his hero Mikhail Yuryevich Lermontov's 'The Sail'. Ivan's response is a warning. Those who seek out violence, as in the poem where the protagonist hopes to find calm in the heart of a storm, will meet a violent end. I use *Three Little Pigs* again, as Chekhov reuses the Krylov, and the huffing and puffing is quite nice for evoking a storm…